Fifty Wonders of Korea

Volume 2. Science and Technology

Edited and Published by

Korean Spirit & Culture Promotion Project

Fifty Wonders of Korea

Volume 2. Science and Technology

Edited and Published by

Korean Spirit & Culture Promotion Project

http://www.kscpp.net

Printed and Bound by

Samjung Munhwasa

Chungjeong-ro 37-18, Seodaemun-gu, Seoul

ISBN: 978-0-9797263-4-7

First print, September 2008

Printed in the Republic of Korea

Contents

Appendix

Contributors of Images

We would like to express our gratitude to the following organizations and individuals for their kind permission to reproduce images in this book.

Cultural Heritage Administration of Korea

Discovery Media

Donga Science Corporation

Ewha Womans University Press

Haman Museum

Hyundai Heavy Industries

Jonginamoo Gallery

Korea Energy Information Center

Korea Tourism Organization

National Museum of Korea

The War Memorial of Korea

Nam Moon-hyon (Professor, Konkuk Univeristy)

Park Chang-bom (Professor, Korean Institute for Advanced Study)

Note on Romanization

The Romanization of Korean words in this book follows the McCune-Reischauer system, except in the case of prominent cultural assets, figures and place names for which alternative usages are better known, and of individuals who have expressed a preference for alternative spellings of their names.

Preface

In the past century, few nations have experienced a history as turbulent and dramatic as that of Korea. Despite Japanese colonization (1910-1945), followed by the Korean War (1950-1953) and the Cold War, and more recently the Asian financial crisis (1997), not to mention the division with the North that remains to this day, South Koreans have made great economic and industrial progress, and achieved remarkable successes in the fields of science and sport, culture and the arts.

One of the world's poorest nations in the early 1960's, South Korea is now recognized by the World Bank as a 'High Income' country, and an 'Advanced Economy' by the International Monetary Fund (IMF) and the USA's Central Intelligence Agency (CIA). It is now the world's 13th largest economy, among the top ten global exporters, and at the forefront of the IT industry. Koreans such as UN Secretary-General Ban Ki-moon, as well as prominent scientists, musicians, artists, and sports icons, are playing an active role on the international stage.

Korean popular culture, including music, movies, and TV dramas, has recently gained huge popularity beyond its neighbors in Asia – a phenomenon known as the *Hallyu* or 'Korean Wave.' As interest in Korea's language, food, fashion, and customs increases, the influence of its culture is growing. How is it that Korea has been able to achieve such an astonishing recovery?

Koreans are known for their strong work ethic and emphasis on the importance of education. The leadership of President Park Chung-hee greatly contributed to the economic development of the country, coinciding with a period of unprecedented growth. On a broader level, however, Korea's progress could be attributed to the tireless and innovative spirit of its ancestors – for the character and potential of a nation is not created in a day.

Fifty Wonders of Korea: Volume 2 attempts to introduce some of the most notable scientific legacies from Korea's past, many of which remain largely unknown to the world. While the first volume dealt with culture and art, the second discusses 30 items of scientific and technological value, ranging from astronomy, meteorology, and medicine, to food, weapons, architecture, and precision craftsmanship.

Korea is home to a number of remarkable inventions. Moveable metal type was in use in Korea 200 years before the well-known printing press of Gutenberg appeared in Germany. Korea also produced the world's oldest woodblock print, as well as the world's oldest star chart and astronomical observatory. It is also credited with the invention of the world's first ironclad warship, timed explosive device, multi-rocket launcher, active greenhouse, rain-gauge, and sand mold, and has developed paper, heating systems, and metal tableware that are among the most sophisticated examples of their kind. Korean food, which includes unique dishes such as kimchi, bulgogi, and other fermented recipes, is famous for its remarkable health benefits, as well as its taste. (Some of the chapters discuss military science, but it should be remembered that the military innovations were made only for the purpose of national defense. There have been numerous foreign invasions throughout Korean history, but Korea has never invaded another country, except for a few expeditions in order to restrain the activities of *wako* pirates.)

Like all nations, Korea's history contains both triumphs and tragedies. The many treasures produced over its long history, however, are worthy of worldwide attention. The rule of King Sejong in the early 15th century was a golden age for Korea. Besides the creation of the native alphabet *Hangul*, great progress was made in the areas of medicine, agriculture, national defense, astronomy, and other sciences. According to a scientific dictionary published in Japan in 1983, 29 of the world's greatest achievements between 1400 and 1450 were made in Korea, while 5 are attributed to China, 0 to Japan, and 28 to the regions outside East Asia, which include the Americas, Europe, and Middle East. This clearly demonstrates the levels to which science and technology were taken under King Sejong, surpassing the achievements of any other nation of the day.

Many of the legacies of Korea's past were destroyed during the Japanese invasion in the 16th century and under its colonization in the early 20th century. In the aftermath of the civil war in the 1950s, all attention and energy was devoted to reconstruction and the revival of the economy. As a result, Koreans have not promoted their history and culture, and research and publications in Western languages covering Korea remain few and far between. It is our hope that this book will place the distinguished heritage of this small but extraordinary nation within the reach of a wider audience.

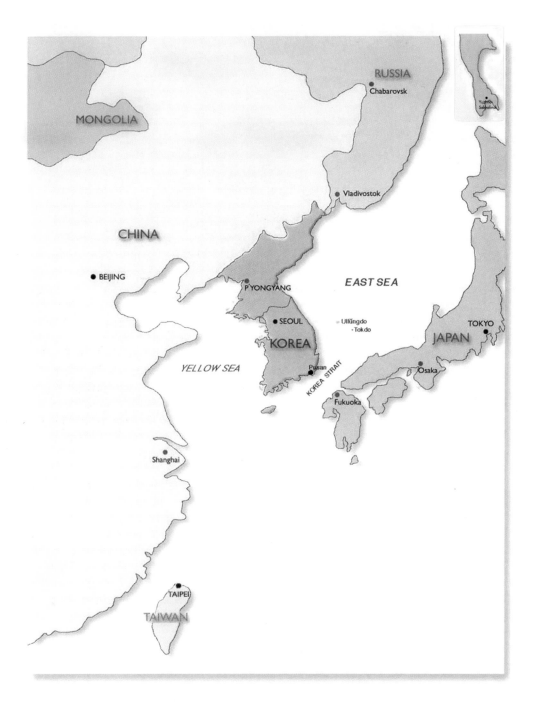

Map of Korea and neighboring countries

Timeline of Korean History

BC 700,000~BC 8000	Paleolithic Period
BC 8000~BC 2000	Neolithic Period
BC 2333~BC 108	Old Choson Dynasty: The First Kingdom of Korea (Bronze Age & Iron Age)
BC 57~AD 668	Three Kingdoms Period: Koguryo, Paekche and Silla
AD 668~AD 935	Unified Silla
AD 918~AD 1392	Koryo Dynasty
AD 1392~AD 1910	Choson Dynasty
AD 1910~AD 1945	Japanese Occupation
AD 1948	Korea divided into North and South
AD 1950~1953	Korean War

Source: National Institute of Korean History (2007)

Human life in the Korean peninsula can be traced back to the Paleolithic era of 700,000 years ago. The roots of Korean culture started to form around BC 8000. Examples of so-called 'comb-pattern' pottery, which began to appear in the peninsula around BC 5000, are among the most well-known and important archeological relics of the Neolithic Age. The first kingdom of Korea was called *Choson* ('Land of Morning Calm'). It was founded by Tangun Wanggum in BC 2333, on the principle of *Hongik Ingan*, which means 'to live and act for the benefit of all mankind.' The two volumes of *Fifty Wonders of Korea* discuss legacies from the Old Choson dynasty (BC 2333~BC 108) through to the later Choson dynasty (AD 1392~AD 1910). All of them are direct and vivid sources of Korea's past, and reflect the diverse colors of Korean culture. Korea was a united country for most of its history, but has been divided into the communist North and the democratic South since 1948. The two Koreas have developed distinct cultures over the last 60 years. Today, North Korea is one of the poorest and most closed societies in the world, while South Korea is among the wealthiest and most advanced.

21. Dolmen Stones

Dolmen stones are mysterious tomb-like structures dating from the bronze and iron ages. They are predominantly found in the East, with the largest portion (two thirds) residing in Korea. Astronomical markings discovered on Korean dolmen stones have been shown to predate the Babylonian constellation drawings, previously thought to be mankind's first astronomical records, by 1800 years. Accurate and comprehensive, they are a tribute to the resourcefulness of ancient Korean astronomers.

Old Choson, the first ancient state of Korea, is known to have existed from the 24th to the 2nd century BC, or in archaeological terms, throughout the Bronze and Iron Ages. It also coincided with the so-called 'megalithic' period, during which dolmens (single chamber structures consisting of vertical and horizontal stones) and menhirs (freestanding boulders) were erected, often for religious reasons. In terms of scientific history, this is when Korean astronomy began.

The Korean peninsula contains about two thirds of the world's dolmens, with at least 50,000 currently known to the academic world. 20,000 of these have been discovered in the Cholla Province alone, the highest density per unit area in the world. In November 2000, the dolmen sites at Ganghwa, Hwasun, and Gochang were included in UNESCO's World Heritage List.

500 dolmens have been discovered in Japan (on the island of Kyushu) and 400 in China (350 in Liaoning Province, 50 in Zhejiang Province). Judging by the proximity of these areas to Korea, it is believed they were influenced by Korea's own culture of dolmen art. In Europe, menhirs predominate, with only a few thousand dolmens discovered so far.

A Dolmen Structure in Mungyong, North Kyongsang Province

Many dolmens are confirmed to have been ancient tombs, but some are thought to have been monuments. Items excavated from those confirmed as tombs include stone axes and arrowheads, lute-shaped bronze daggers, and various earthenware and jade items. In most cases, the cover stone weighs less than 10 tons, with the larger ones generally weighing between 20-40 tons. The heaviest known cover stone in the Korean peninsula weighs 102 tons and is from Roam-ri, South Hwanghae Province. It measures $9.10 \times 6.40 \times 0.70 \text{m}^3$, giving a total volume of 40.8m^3.

The Babylonian boundary-stones of Mesopotamia, with engraved images of dogs, snakes, scorpions, and other symbolic creatures, were generally believed to be mankind's earliest depictions of the stars. Hence, the Mesopotamian region has been regarded as the birthplace of ancient astronomy, and one of the four cradles of human civilization.

However, recent research has confirmed that images of constellations found

on dolmens near the Taedong River date from 3000 BC, preceding the Babylonian charts by some 1800 years. In his book *The Seven Wonders of Korea*, Professor Lee Jong-ho claims "The dolmen constellations provide concrete evidence that the ancient Koreans were leaders in cultural development together with the four cradles of civilization, and that these constellations are a significant scientific heritage, on a scale comparable to the wonders of the world."

The dolmens with engravings of astronomical charts are found mostly in Pyongyang, and number around 200. Before it was discovered that the holes on the surface of the dolmens represented stars, views differed as to what they might be. Some saw them as an expression of the worship of the sun or the heavens, while others associated them with funeral ceremonies. Some interpreted them as denoting the frequency of a certain ancestral rite, or the number of animals offered for sacrifice. Close examination of the arrangement of holes, however, revealed they were a representation of the constellations around the North Star.

The most well-known of these constellation patterns is found on the surface of a dolmen from Woesae Mountain in the South Pyongan Province. The cover stone of the dolmen tomb bears 80 holes, with a central hole representing the North Pole, and the others making up 11 different constellations. The size of the holes also varies throughout according to luminosity (brighter stars are larger), and when the observations were dated, taking the precession of equinoxes into account, it was determined that they represented the night sky from 2800 BC[1].

Constellation patterns found on a dolmen stone from the Pyongwon district in the South Pyongan Province were estimated to have been inscribed around 2500 BC, whilst the dolmen constellation found in the Hamju district of the South Hamgyong Province is dated to 1500 BC. When we look at the latter chart from the Hamju district, we can see that it is more accurate than the maps from previous eras. For instance, the holes corresponding to Great Bear and the Little Bear are more accurately distanced with reference to the pole star than in the Pyongwon chart, and stars down to the 4th-magnitude have been included.

In total, 40 constellations are displayed on the 200 dolmens in the valley of the Taedong River, including 28 from the regions around the pole star, skyline and equator. These include all the constellations visible at night from Pyongyang at 39 degrees north latitude, as well as the Milky Way and clusters of the Pleiades (the Seven Sisters). The charting of so many stars, before the invention of telescopes, is an unmatched feat in the history of astronomy.

Dolmen constellations have also been discovered in the southern Korean peninsula. In 1978, Professor Lee Yung-jo discovered a small stone tablet

---

[1] ±220 years

(23.5cm wide, 32.5cm long) in a dolmen site submerged in the Taechong Dam in North Chungchong Province. The tablet bears 65 small and large holes, between 2cm and 7cm in diameter. Through computer simulation, Professor Park Chang-bom of the Korea Institute for Advanced Study established that it was an astronomical chart from 500 BC, depicting constellations such as the Big Dipper, the Little Dipper, the Dragon and Cassiopeia.

It is not certain why constellation maps were carved upon the dolmen tomb stones, but the general consensus is that ancient beliefs about death were linked to the worship of the heavens. This is also demonstrated by the fact that almost all the cover stones with astronomical markings are fashioned in the shape of a turtle's back. The turtle was revered by Koreans as one of the Ten Symbols of Longevity, and was believed to represent eternal youth. By making tombstones in the shape of a turtle, the people of ancient Korea believed they could enjoy a long life in the afterworld, and receive protection from the Turtle God. Representative of Korea's prehistoric era, and recording something of the knowledge and culture of the age, the dolmens are an important part of the ancient history of East Asia.

22. Kingdom of Astronomy

The history of astronomy in Korea is rich and varied, with over 20,000 observations of astronomical phenomena accumulated over the course of 2,000 years. These records are a valuable source for modern astronomers, firstly for their historical reach, and secondly for their reliability. Of the main nations of East Asia, for example, Korean records of solar eclipses show the highest rate of accuracy.

The history of classical Korean astronomy spans over two millennia. Evidence of this past can still be seen today, such as *Chomsongdae*, the world's oldest surviving observatory, and the star maps from the megalithic and Three Kingdoms period. Formal astronomical science reached its zenith under King Sejong in the 15th century, leaving behind a wealth of observational data.

Observing and recording the movements of the heavenly bodies is fundamental to the study of astronomy, as it only becomes possible to identify patterns and recurrences, and thus to understand the laws that govern the universe, after studying astronomical phenomena over long periods of time.

Ancient Korean kingdoms established their own departments of astronomy, with observatories and officials dedicated to observing phenomena. Official observation of the sky began in the 1st century BC. The number of astronomical phenomena recorded in the major historical texts from different eras, including the *History of the Three Kingdoms, Memorabilia of the Three Kingdoms, History of Koryo,* and *Royal Annals of the Choson Dynasty*, amount to over 20,000 records in total. These include solar eclipses, eclipses of planets by the moon, planetary movements, comets, changes in the brightness of planets, meteors, meteorites and meteoric showers, auroras, and rare appearances of southern stars.

Such thorough observations and records provide important material for modern scientific research. Accounts of solar and lunar eclipses, for example, reveal long-term changes in the earth's revolution and its rotational velocity. Records of the moon obscuring planets can be used to measure irregular lunar motion, while records indicate the evolution of long-period comets and the existence of short-period comets that have now disappeared. Together with accounts of meteors and meteorites, the records reveal spatial changes in the solar system that have taken place over thousands of years. Furthermore, records of auroras provide information on movements in the earth's magnetic field and changes in solar activity over long periods of time.

Today, there are computer programs that can simulate the motions of celestial bodies in the very distant past and show us the sky as it appeared at a given point in time, and from a particular place. With the aid of such software, we can calculate the movements of the sun and the moon, and recreate solar eclipses that happened thousands of years ago. The modern astronomer Park Changbom calculated the celestial dynamics around Korea and the neighboring countries, and sought to verify whether the recorded solar eclipses had taken place[1].

The *History of the Three Kingdoms* contains 67 records of solar eclipses from 54 BC to 911 AD. Of these, 53 (79%) have been verified to have taken place. Until the early third century AD, the percentage of proven records was higher at 89%. In the case of China, the verification rate was at its highest during the Han dynasty (78%), and afterwards remained between 63%~75% until the Tang dynasty. From its first observation of a solar eclipse in 638 AD until 950 AD, Japan's early records exhibit a real occurrence rate of 35%.

---

[1] A more detailed discussion of this study may be found in the research papers of Park Changbom and La Daile. Park Changbom, La Daile, "Verification of the Independence of the Astronomical Observations in the time of Three Kingdoms", Journal of the Korean History of Science Society, Vol. 16 (1994).

As far as solar eclipses are concerned, the *History of the Three Kingdoms* is the most credible among the contemporary historical records of Northeast Asia, the region with the richest astronomical heritage in the world.

Astronomical Heritage of Korea

Dates	Period	Astronomical Heritage
30C BC~ AD 2C	Stone, Bronze & Iron Age	Petroglyphs, constellations of dolmens, menhirs, and burial items
24C BC~ 2C BC	Old Choson	12 astronomical records Chamsongdan observatory at Mt. Manisan, Kanghwado
57 BC~AD 935 37 BC~AD 668 18 BC~AD 660*	Silla Koguryo Paekche	Over 240 astronomical records in *History of the Three Kingdoms* and *Memorabilia of the Three Kingdoms* 25 Koguryo tomb murals depicting star maps *Chomsongdae* observatory in Kyongju established (observatory survives to this day) Sundials, statues of four-directional animals**, 12 zodiacal animal deities
918~1392	Koryo	Over 5,000 astronomical records in *History of Koryo* *Chomsongdang* observatory in Kaesong 9 Koryo tomb murals depicting star maps
1392~1910	Choson	Over 15,000 astronomical records in the *Royal Annals of the Choson Dynasty, Diaries of the Royal Secretariat,* and *Daily Records of the Stars* Astronomical installations, e.g. observatories, armillary spheres, and celestial globes Astronomical literature, charts Timekeeping devices such as sundials, clepsydrae (water clocks), and astronomical clocks

* The periods of the three kingdoms overlap, as they existed simultaneously and covered different parts of Korea.
** The four mythical animals in East Asian tradition that represent the four points of the compass: Blue Dragon (East), White Tiger (West), Red Phoenix (South), Half-Turtle, Half-Serpent (North).

23. Noteworthy Astronomical Records

Ancient Korean astronomical data is still used in research today, as it gives us valuable information about cosmic events that occurred before the use of telescopes. The records of sunspots and auroras were detailed enough to allow conclusions to be drawn about astronomical cycles that have only recently become established theories. Comets were also faithfully observed; for example, Korea possesses the most exhaustive account of a comet appearance ever written. Reports of meteors and meteoric showers also provide astronomers with an insight into the evolution of the solar system.

Korea's ancient and medieval kingdoms produced a considerable amount of astronomical data over the centuries, some of which is still being used in today's research. In this chapter, we examine a few of the most notable examples.

Sunspots and Auroras

The records of sunspots and auroras, which show how solar activity, solar wind, and the geomagnetic field have changed over long periods of time, are useful for the study of the solar system and the Earth. The sun has only been regularly observed with telescopes for the past 300 years. In order to trace long-term changes over thousands of years, it is necessary to refer to observations made with the naked eye that have been preserved in historical records.

The observation of sunspots began properly in Europe in 1611 with the studies of Johann Fabricius and Galileo Galilei. In Asia, both China and Korea possessed long-term records of sunspots going back many hundreds of years. For

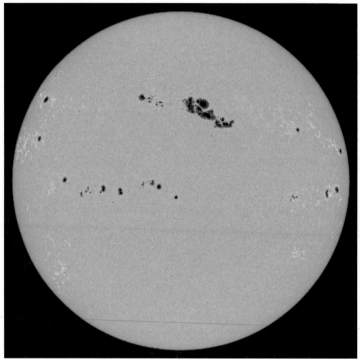

Photograph of a large sunspot taken March 29, 2001
(SOHO satellite photo)

example, a record from Koguryo in 640 AD says, "The light of the sun disappeared and did not return for three days," and one from Silla in 822 AD says, "A vertical strip of black appeared on the sun." During the Koryo period, 35 unambiguous records of sunspots are preserved, beginning with an entry in 1151 AD, "There is a black spot on the sun, about the size of an egg." At the time, sunspots were generally called *heukja* (literally 'black spot') and for consistency, size was indicated with reference to the objects plum, egg, peach, and pear.

An aurora is a display of light that occurs when high-energy particles released during solar activity collide with particles in the Earth's magnetosphere. Korea left more records of auroras than any other country, with more than 700 documented up to the mid-18th century. These records are impressive not merely for their number, but also for their accuracy.

An aurora with red and green lights, observed near the Big Dipper
(Dover, Oklahoma, October 29, 2003.)

Magnetic storms can be repetitive or non-repetitive. Non-repetitive magnetic storms occur frequently one to two years after a solar maximum, leading to a strong aurora; in contrast, repetitive magnetic storms occur soon after a solar minimum and are weak. This fact only became established in the late 20th century, but 800 years earlier, Korean astronomers had collected the data necessary for this conclusion.

The Korean records of sunspots and auroras are particularly valuable because they clearly show an 11-year cycle in solar activity, not found in the contemporary records of other countries. The 11-year Sunspot Cycle was established by the German astronomer Samuel Heinrich Schwabe in 1843, and later a corresponding cycle in the frequency and strength of auroras was also discovered. If equivalent analytical tools had been available to Koryo astronomers, the details of the cycle of solar activity might have been discovered some 500 years earlier.

Comets

The observation and documentation of comets in Korea was also conducted over a long period of time. The report of a large comet in 1664 is the most notable example: it was placed under daily observation for 80 days (although invisible for eight days due to cloud cover) from the tenth month of 1664 to the first month of 1665. Besides mapping out the nearby constellations and the path taken by the comet, the report also records the rank and the signatures of the recording astronomers. Described by the Japanese astronomer

Halley's Comet

Wada Yuji as 'an incomparable treasure in the history of astronomy,' it is regarded as the most comprehensive account of a comet's appearance ever written.

One of the most famous comets is the eponymous 'Halley's Comet', named after the British astronomer Edmond Halley, who argued in a paper published in 1705 that the comet he had seen in 1682 was the same as had appeared previously in 1607 and 1531, and forecast that it would appear again in 1758. From 989 in the early Koryo period to 1835 in the late Choson period, appearances of this comet were recorded consistently. The detailed reports note the time the comet appeared, its location, any changes in its form, its color and size, the length of its tail, the date of disappearance, and the names of the officials who observed it. The Department of Astronomy in its official chronicles reports, "The light of the comet is a reflection of the sun. When the comet appears at night the tail points to the east, and when it appears at dawn, it points to the west." From this we see that the link between the sun and the direction of a comet's tail was understood.

From the records of Korea, China, and Japan, we learn of many other short-term periodic comets that existed in the past, and also how long-term periodic comets over the past 2,000 years have changed orbit or sublimated (changed from solid to gaseous form) as they approach the sun.

Falling Stars and Meteoric Showers

There is a great deal of matter in the solar system besides the planets and their satellites. Some are relatively large objects such as asteroids, but many are smaller, such as blocks of ice or rocks shed by passing comets. Some of these objects, known as meteors, enter the earth's atmosphere and start to burn. Some of these meteors, known as 'falling stars' or more properly 'meteorites', reach the ground before they disintegrate.

In Korea, the earliest record of a falling star is in the year 14 AD. The first record of a meteoric shower is in 104 AD. The *History of Koryo* contains records of 740 occurrences of falling stars and meteoric showers. In the Choson dynasty, there are as many as 3,111 recorded occurrences in the *Royal Annals of the Choson Dynasty*. Because such phenomena could be seen almost every day, however, in 1490 the annals declared that only special cases would be recorded in the future.

By examining the times of year when falling stars and meteoric showers were most frequently observed in the Koryo and Choson dynasties, we can learn how the solar system has changed. According to records, the largest number of falling stars could be seen on the twenty-fifth day of the seventh month. This was the day when the earth passed through the meteoroid stream of the Swift-Tuttle comet, and a meteor shower known today as the Perseids occurred. Many meteors were also observed around the end of the tenth month, today known as the Leonids, although this was not as intense as the Perseids. A comparison of Koryo and Choson records shows that the Leonids appeared ten days later during the Choson period, that is, early in the eleventh month rather than late in the tenth. The old records therefore indicate how the solar system environment, filled with the debris of comets, has evolved over the past thousand years.

24. The World's Oldest Surviving Observatory

Koreans paid close attention to celestial phenomena, as they believed that events in the sky were a mirror and guide for earthly affairs. *Chomsongdae*, the world's oldest observatory, was built during the Silla period, and is rich in astronomical symbolism as well as being carefully designed for its scientific purpose. Built in the palace grounds, it was tall enough to offer a wide and unobstructed view of the heavens.

Why did Koreans observe and document celestial phenomena so carefully? As a society, they believed that man should live in harmony with Nature. In the official *History of Koryo* (918~1392), there is a section entitled the *Book of Astronomy* which provides 5,000 highly reliable astronomical records taken during the dynasty. The foreword to the book states the reason for its publication as follows:

> With signs thus expressed, the Heavens show fortune and misfortune,
> And the wise will give heed to what they show.

The belief expressed here is that the Heavens are like a mirror reflecting the human world, and they reveal good and evil through events and transformations in the celestial world. Therefore, the wise always pay attention to the Heavens as the world's reflection, and try to understand its meaning and humbly follow its will.

Koreans therefore went to great lengths to study the movements of celestial bodies and the various phenomena in the sky. Through unceasing observation

***Chomsongdae* in Kyongju**
Height 9.5m, built around AD 632, National Treasure No. 31

and calculation, they established astronomy as an academic tradition.

Chomsongdae is a legacy that embodies this ancient astronomical tradition. *Chomsongdae* literally means 'a platform for observing the stars', and is the world's oldest extant observatory. It was built inside the royal palace grounds during the Silla dynasty around 632 AD, during the reign of Queen Sondok. Modeled on an observatory in the kingdom of Paekche, which now exists only in historical records, *Chomsongdae's* design was later used as the basis for the observatory in Asuka, Japan in 675 AD, and Duke Zhou's observatory in China in 723 AD.

This serene and beautiful building was designed with great care and thought, so that the parts and the whole both carried an astronomical meaning. *Chomsongdae's* square summit and circular body reflect the traditional concept that the sky is round and the earth is square. The structure comprises 29 layers of stone, corresponding to the 29.5 days in a lunar month counted from one crescent moon to the next. The 27 layers of the cylindrical body represent the time taken for the moon to revolve once around the earth (27.3 days). There are 12 layers of stone above and below the window at the center of the observatory, symbolizing the 12 months of the year, and together representing the 24 seasonal divisions. The number of stone slabs supporting the structure at the base is also 12.

In the upper part of the main body, there are 6 protruding stone slabs that aid structural stability. Besides these stones, the total number of stone slabs used in the round body is 364. The 27th layer (the top of the body) is a horizontal slab, raising the total to 365, the number of days in a year.

At 9.5 meters, the observatory is much taller than the surviving observatories of the later dynasties of Koryo and Choson. Records state that it was designed to be climbed from the inside, and it is believed entry was gained via the middle window by means of a ladder placed outside. Once inside, another ladder was used to gain access to the summit, where astronomical observations were made.

Indeed, there are clear indentation marks on either side at the bottom of the window, indicating that a thick wooden ladder was once installed there.

Modern astronomical observatories are usually built in mountain locations. It may therefore seem strange that this observatory was established in the heart of Kyongju, the Silla capital. Professor Nam Chun-woo of Seoul National University has suggested that observatories are located in remote regions nowadays because the artificial light in city areas is too strong during the night, and that numerous dust particles in the polluted air obscure the stars. 1,400 years ago in Kyongju, however, there was neither light pollution nor air pollution, and it was possible to observe the stars from level ground. In the event of extraordinary astronomical phenomena that needed to be reported immediately to the king, it was ideal for the observatory to be located inside the palace grounds.

At the same time, the height of *Chomsongdae* (9.5m) is sufficient to command an unobstructed view of the skies, regardless of nearby trees or buildings. The view is not obscured by trees shorter than 9m in the immediate vicinity. Likewise a tree 15m tall at a distance of 50m, or a 20m tree at a distance of 100m, is visible only at an angle of elevation of 6 degrees or less. The *Chomsongdae* observatory was therefore of an ideal height to observe the stars.

25. The Legacy of Koguryo

Koguryo, one of the Three Kingdoms of Korea, left behind many stone-chamber murals depicting star patterns. Its most important legacy is a star map confirmed as the oldest complete representation of the skies in the world. It lies hidden within a later Choson star map, based upon the Koguryo original, but its true age and origins can be inferred from the stellar positions.

Traditional Korean astronomy began during the megalithic period (Old Choson), and its accumulated tradition carried down to the period of the Three Kingdoms. Koguryo (37 BC-AD 668) built stone-chamber tombs for their dead, sometimes decorating them with elaborate murals. Many studies have been conducted on these tomb murals, which are valuable not only for their superb artistry, but also for the information they provide about the culture of the day.

A total of 25 Koguryo tombs are known to feature murals depicting stars or whole constellations. The constellations were generally expressed by using lines to connect the stars, and hence are invaluable records for studying the night sky of ancient East Asia. As seen in Tokhwa-ri Tomb No. 2 and Chinpa-ri Tomb No. 4, some star maps differentiated the brightness of stars by size, a custom also found on dolmen stones.

Another important legacy of the astronomy of Koguryo can be found on the planispheric[3] star map entitled *Chonsang yolcha punya chido* (literally 'the natural order of the heavenly bodies and the regions they govern'). Designated National Treasure No. 228 of Korea, it was inscribed on a black marble in 1395, four years after Taejo founded the Choson dynasty (1392~1910). According to

---

[3] A planisphere is projection of a sphere (or part of a sphere) onto a plane surface.

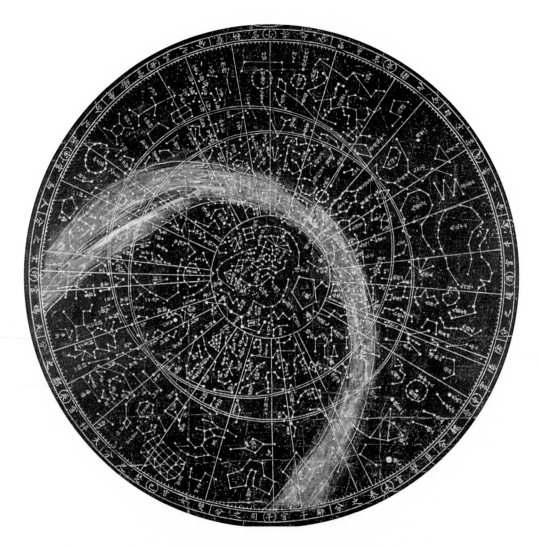

Rubbed copy of the *Chonsang yolcha punya chido*

Collection of Sungshin Women's University Museum

the explanation on the marble: 'There was a rock-engraved constellation chart in Koguryo's Pyongyang Fortress, but it was lost during the Chinese invasion and only a rubbed copy remains. This constellation chart is based on the extant copy.' This means that what was recorded on the Koguryo constellation chart can also be seen in the planisphere which copied it, and it depicts all 1,467 stars visible to the naked eye from the Korean peninsula.

Based on its date of production, it is known as the world's second oldest star map engraved in stone, next to China's Suzhou Star Chart of 1247. However, this description is inaccurate. Since the time period implied by the stellar positions on the map is the first century AD, this makes it the oldest complete representation of the sky in the world, and therefore a rare scientific artifact. The date of observation is validated not only by historical records but also by the stellar positions themselves, which enable us to infer the point from which the observations must have been made.

The Earth's axis of rotation describes a 'circumpolar' circle in the sky every 25,800 years, and the position of the earth changes with respect to the constellations. This is referred to as the 'precession of the equinoxes'. We can use this fact to ascertain the date a celestial map was made, by comparing the stellar positions depicted on the map with the current position of the North Pole and the equator. When the epoch of the constellation chart on the *Chonsang yolcha punya chido* was determined using this method, the positions of the circumpolar stars in the center corresponded to their positions in the early Choson dynasty in the 14th century, whilst the majority of the stars outside the circumpolar circle matched those of the 1st century, 2,000 years ago. The region around the North Pole on the map, the reference point for measuring latitudes and hence drawing star maps, is marked at 38° north latitude, which corresponds to Hanyang (Seoul), the capital of Choson. The region of the stars enclosed by the outer circles of the map is marked at 39-40° north latitude, corresponding to Koguryo, which occupied the northern part of the Korean peninsula and much of southern Manchuria.

The star map on the ceiling of Kitora Tomb in the village of Asuka Japan is assumed to have been made in the late 7th century, and is further evidence of the astronomical knowledge of Koguryo and its influence on neighboring countries. Discovered in 1998 during an inspection of the tomb's interior, the Kitora star map depicts all the constellations except those only visible from the South Pole, as well as the sun and moon and the four directional animals[4].

According to Japanese astronomical historians Professor Hashimoto and Miyajima, the base of observation for this chart was 38.4° north latitude. This latitude is much closer to Pyongyang, the capital of Koguryo (39°), than to Asuka (34.5°). The Koguryo origin of the Kitora star map is further corroborated by the fact that the tomb lies a mere 1.2km away from the well-known Takamastu tomb, in which a mural painting depicting a group of ladies in Koguryo style costume was found. It is believed by scholars that the murals were a legacy of Koguryo immigrants, who sought sanctuary in Japan after the defeat of Koguryo by Silla in 668 AD. A study of the positioning of the stars depicted in the Kitora chart has also confirmed that it is a projection of the heavens some two millennia ago, which corresponds to the early Koguryo period, like the *Chonsang yolcha punya chido*.

---

[4] See note on page 18.

26. Astronomy under King Sejong

The construction of an advanced astronomical observatory under King Sejong in 1438 meant that eclipses could be predicted with accuracy to the very second of their occurrence. As well as enabling national ceremonies to be performed without error, the new observatory made it possible to calculate calendar periods correctly to six significant figures. As a result, Korea was one of only three 15th century nations able to calculate the movements of the planets with respect to their own latitude of observation.

Korean astronomy entered a new era of precision under King Sejong (1397~1450), and calendrical science also developed greatly. In 1438 a large observatory was built in the garden of Kyonghoe Pavilion at Kyongbok Palace. The observatory was 9.5m high, 14.4m long and 9.8m wide. On the roof were installed various astronomical instruments such as an armillary sphere [5] (*honchonui*), a celestial globe, giving a spherical model of the heavens, (*honsang*), and a gnomon (*gyupyo*), a device for measuring the altitude of the sun. With these instruments, the sky could be observed in great detail. When this installation was completed, after seven years of extensive work beginning in 1432, the Choson royal family had within their palace walls the most advanced astronomical facilities of the 15th century. The *Royal Annals* (*Sillok*) document this historic moment in great detail, and we gather that the historians who recorded it were proud of its successful inauguration. Officials from the Hall of Heavenly Records, in charge of astronomy and meteorology, took observations

---

[5] A system of circular bands surrounding a representation of the Earth, and corresponding to the tracks of various celestial bodies around it.

there every day. When unusual celestial phenomena such as eclipses or comets were seen, a report was prepared for immediate dispatch to the Royal Secretariat and other major government offices. Regrettably, the observatory was completely destroyed during the Japanese invasion of the late 16th century, and no trace of the original building remains.

During the Choson dynasty (1392~1910), when heavenly omens such as solar or lunar eclipses occurred, the King performed a ceremony known as *kusikrye*, in order to interpret the will of the heavens and determine an appropriate course of action. This was a very important ceremony in the Confucian society of Choson, which emphasized the importance of mankind living in harmony with nature and fulfilling its allotted role within the cosmic and social order. It was therefore the duty of appointed officials to carefully observe the celestial phenomena, record any changes, and also give the monarch three months notice before such phenomena were expected to occur again.

For the sake of ceremonial order, it was necessary for the predicted time to be accurate to the minute and second. If the predicted time proved wrong, the officials of the Hall of Heavenly Records would face punishment. From 1438 onwards, thanks to the accumulation of knowledge and the development of various astronomical instruments and time-signaling devices, the solar and lunar eclipses could be predicted with precision, and the ceremonies performed without error.

In the past, the length of a day, month, and year were determined according to the cyclical motions of the sun and moon. A day was the time taken for the sun to rise and cross the meridian, a lunar month was the time taken for a new moon to circle the earth, and a solar year was the time taken for all the four seasons to pass. However, the solar year is not an integral multiple[6] of the lunar month, and neither the lunar month nor the solar year is an integral multiple of a

---

[6] The number of lunar months in a solar year is a number with a fraction, not a "whole" number.

Model of armillary sphere '*Honchonui*' at the royal tomb of King Sejong

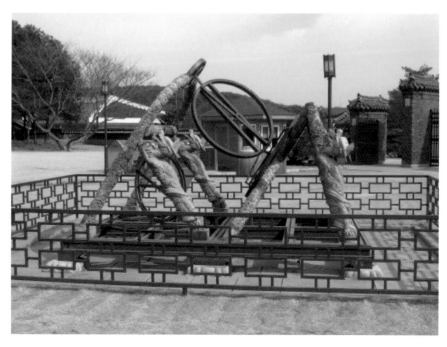

Model of astronomical instrument '*Kanui*' at the royal tomb of King Sejong

solar day. The calendar method of expressing a date as a certain day of a certain month of a certain year is intrinsically imperfect. Therefore, all throughout history it has been necessary to adjust calendars after a certain period of time has passed.

The lunar calendar traditionally used by Korea and other Asian countries follows the movement of the moon, with the occasional addition of a leap month to adjust for the seasons. It is therefore a luni-solar calendar. In contrast, the Gregorian calendar, currently the world's standard, is a solar calendar that follows the changing of the seasons, and does not take the lunar cycles into account. Though very accurate, it is also imperfect and makes use of a leap year about every four years, and nowadays leap seconds are added as well.

As calendrical astronomy was a matter of national importance, King Sejong made exceptions in both rank and procedure in order to appoint the best minds in the kingdom to take charge. He himself studied the Xuanming calendar from Tang China and compared it with the Shoushi calendar from Yuan China, together with many other books related to astronomy and the calendar, in order to produce a calendar of Korea's own. In addition, he took detailed observations of solar and lunar eclipses and compared his observations with the forecasts of existing calendars to assess their accuracy. These efforts of Sejong required great patience, as they were made over a long period of time. The following record from the 12th year of his reign speaks of his difficulties with the subject, and his determination to resolve the matter.

'To understand the principles of calendrical science and astronomy is very difficult. Let us once again study the method of calculation, compose a draft and then wait, as someone who knows the field very well will surely appear in the future.'

- *Sejong Sillok*, 11th day of 12th month, 1430

Next year, Sejong ordered Chong In-ji, Chong Cho, and Chong Heum-ji to develop a calendrical method that would facilitate accurate calculation of the movements of the heavenly bodies. The following 12 years of labor and research came to fruition in a work entitled *A Calculation of the Movements of the Seven Celestial Determinants* (1442). It was a landmark in the history of astronomical science, including details of the movements of the sun and moon, as well as Mars, Mercury, Jupiter, Venus, and Saturn. It fully incorporated the calendrical theories of China and Arabia, adjusting them with reference to the latitude of Seoul. As a result, Choson astronomers were able to calculate the position of all the planets with respect to the Korean capital, as well as the times of sunrise and sunset, and solar and lunar eclipses. The book calculates one year to be 365.2425 days, and one month to be 29.530593 days, values correct to six significant figures according to modern calculations.

A Calculation of the Movements of the Seven Celestial Determinants is regarded as one of the most remarkable astronomical achievements of its day. The work was introduced to Japan by an envoy named Pak In-gi in the 17th century, and Japan later published its own astronomical calendar. When the book was completed in 1442, however, only Korea, China, and Arabia were able to compute celestial phenomena to such a high degree of accuracy, and with respect to their own latitude.

27. A Bronze Mirror

An ornate mirror, made over 2,300 years ago and now designated as a national treasure, conveys with its intricate and miniscule detail the centuries of progress in metal craftsmanship that preceded it. With over 13,000 lines engraved upon its tiny surface, 0.3mm apart and 0.07mm deep, it would have taken the best part of a lifetime to complete. Many failed attempts have been made to recreate it, and the techniques used to decorate the mirror have remained a mystery until very recently.

At Sungsil University Museum, Seoul, there is an ancient relic from the 4th century BC. Its name, *Chanmuni*, means a finely-decorated mirror, referring to the delicate geometric patterns on its surface. It is made of bronze, and has a diameter of 21.2cm. Discovered in South Chungchong Province in the 1960s, it is designated National Treasure No. 141.

The intricacy and minute scale of the geometric design and molding technology represent the culmination of centuries of metal craftsmanship. The diameter of this bronze-mirror is no more than the span of a palm, yet on its surface we find elaborate engravings, consisting of more than 13,000 separate lines. The distance between each line is just 0.3mm. The thickness of the line and the tread is approximately 0.22mm, and the tread itself is about 0.07mm deep. No part of the mirror is left undecorated.

Given this level of precision and detail, it would not be an easy task for a professional technician to replicate the mirror on a drafting board, even with modern equipment. And yet, the mirror's delicate designs were originally achieved by a casting technique, melting bronze and pouring it into a mold,

***Chanmuni* Bronze Mirror**
BC 4th century, Diameter 21.2 cm, Sungsil University Museum

which would naturally have been harder to manage with precision. How was it possible for craftsmen in the 4th century BC to produce such a work, and how long would it have taken? In an age without magnifiers or precision tools, the craftsman must presumably have made his own drawing instruments, and the work must have taken the greater part of his lifetime to complete, even if he was very skilled.

Similar fine-patterned mirrors are found all over the Korean peninsula, as well as in Manchuria and some parts of Japan where Koreans lived during ancient times. The fact that they are not found in China indicates that these mirrors are part of Korea's unique bronze heritage. Around a hundred examples have been excavated to date, and National Treasure No. 141 is the largest and the most exquisite of them all. The mirror can therefore be seen as a true masterpiece of an advanced molding technique and refined aesthetics.

Bronze is an alloy of copper and tin. Because pure copper is too soft, tin has to be added in order to harden it. The hardness is greatest when the tin composition is 28%, but at this level the alloy is too brittle and the mirror breaks easily. Therefore, an appropriate ratio must be used. Analysis of the mirror reveals its tin content is 26.7%. This ratio increases the mirror's hardness sufficiently, and also improves its light reflectivity.

To date, there have been numerous efforts to recreate National Treasure No. 141. Attempts to make a wax mold by engraving designs on to copperplate, lead, or mud, have met with little success, and copies made using this method have always been inferior to the original. In 2006, Professor Kwak Dong-hae of Dongguk University announced that he had finally succeeded in reproducing the mirror, using an ancient technique of coating the mold with pine soot. The pine soot acts as a natural version of today's chemical agents, allowing the casting to be extracted from its mold without damaging the surface. A single application of the pine soot coating will last for a long time, and the same mold can therefore be used to produce many casts. In its day, this feature of pine soot coating allowed mass production of bronze swords to become possible, and placed the benefits of bronzeware items within the reach of a greater number of people.

28. Copper Alloys

Korea was well known for the quality of its copper alloys. Korean bronze was often imported by the Chinese, world leaders in bronze craftsmanship themselves. In the 10th century Korean craftsmen were the first to combine bronze with zinc, an alloy not previously achieved due to zinc's low boiling point. This pioneering spirit paved the way for later and greater innovations in metalwork.

The invention of bronze signaled a new era in the history of mankind. In East Asia, Korea's bronze culture played a major role, giving it significant influence on neighboring countries. *Compendium of Materia Medica*, written by Li Shizhen of Ming China in the late 16th century, is an extensive treatise on natural history and widely regarded as a masterpiece of classical science. In a chapter dealing with metals, the author asserts that Persian copper (brass) is suitable for mirrors, but that Silla copper (bronze) is superior for casting bells. The bronze of Koryo is given similar praise in the *Poetical Essay Concerning Choson* by Dong Yue, who visited the country as an official envoy from Ming China in 1488. In *History of Koryo*, there are also several references to the Chinese importing Koryo bronze. It was not because China was in short supply that they purchased bronze from Koryo, but because the Koryo copper alloy was of such a high quality that special efforts were made to procure it.

The bronze buttons excavated from a dolmen site near Pyongyang date to the 25th century BC, and are the earliest example of bronze craftsmanship in East Asia. At this point in history, bronze was used widely in the production of ritual items, farming tools, weapons, and armor. Modern analysis of a Korean bronze

Bronze Dagger
Bronze Age, Height 42.0cm, National Museum of Korea (Seoul)

dagger produced during the Old Choson period (BC 2333~BC 108) reveals a mixture of copper, tin, and lead in an average ratio of 75: 15: 10, and a remarkable uniformity throughout. Similarly, when the alloy structure of a 2nd century BC bronzeware item was examined, the arrangement of metal particles was found to be unusually regular.

Korean metalworkers were pioneering in their use of new materials. They were among the first craftsmen to attempt an alloy of zinc and bronze. Zinc has a very low melting point (419°C), and due to its high fluidity and low viscosity, it can be easily re-cast. However, it boils at 907°C, and as it is necessary for a zinc-bronze alloy to be heated and liquefied at 1000°C as part of the casting process, finding a method of adding the zinc to bronze is difficult. Nevertheless, the Bronze Age craftsmen of Korea were able to overcome this issue. In the case of a 10th century BC bronze bell, excavated in the North Hamgyong Province, we find that it contains 53.9% copper, 22.3% tin, 13.7% zinc, 5.2% lead, and 4.9% other materials. A mirror and axe unearthed in the Hwanghae Province, both from the Late Bronze Age, contain 7.4% and 24.5% quantities of zinc respectively. This innovative spirit and cumulative expertise in metal craftsmanship would later lead to the invention of moveable metal type, Bangjja bronzeware, and exquisite artworks such as bronze bells.

29. Invention of Sand Molds

The development from fixed type to moveable type in the 11th century AD in Korea was the first major step in the history of printing since the invention of woodblock printing in the 8th century AD. The next, and most important step, was the invention of moveable metal type in the 13th century. The process of producing these types required a new kind of mold in which to cast the metal. Only the sand mold was capable of achieving this, before the advent of metal molds. Early metal types in Western Europe were also made with this method, indicating a possible link between the development of Western and Eastern printing.

In East Asia, books began to be printed around the 8th century AD, initially with the use of woodblocks. Woodblock prints of Buddhist scriptures played a significant role in the lives of Koreans, particularly during the Koryo period when all existing texts were inscribed on a series of more than 80,000 woodblocks called the *Tripitaka Koreana,* now housed at Haeinsa Temple.

During this period in East Asia, the increasing demand for books led to the invention of various moveable typefaces. In the 11th century, a Chinese craftsman called Pi Sheng invented a form of moveable type using ceramics, but due to the weakness of the type material and difficulties involved in making suitable inks, it was never used. In the same period, Koreans began to use moveable wooden types. In the 13th century, woodblock and moveable wooden type were superseded by moveable bronze type. This new printing method was used in Korea for the first time in the world, and was the most important step in the development of printing technology.

The use of metallic type requires special ink, durable paper capable of sustaining the pressure of the type, and developed casting techniques. Korea produced paper and oil-based ink of a high quality that was often exported to neighboring countries. They were also experienced in minting bronze coins and casting letters on bronze bells. But in order to produce a large number of metal types, engraved with small and often complex characters, a more advanced molding-technique was needed. The limited variety of molds then in use were hardly adequate for the task.

A new technique was therefore invented to solidify molten bronze inside greensand molds. This is in line with the conclusion reached by modern scientists who maintain that before the use of metal-molds, the only variety capable of casting metal types was the sand-mold. The technical specifications of these molds have been documented in *Yongjae Chonghwa* by the Koryo scholar Song Hyon (1439~1504), widely viewed as the oldest and the most accurate account of sand-molds. According to the book, the character was carved out on a wood blank, and the wooden type was then pressed against a sand matrix. Metallic bronze was poured into the impressions in the sand to form a piece of type. The rough type was then polished for final shaping.

There remains clear evidence that the early metal types in Western Europe were also made from sand-molds. On this basis, some scholars have suggested the possibility that Gutenberg's printing press was not an independent invention, but was in fact influenced by Korea.[7] However, no further research has been conducted on this issue.

---

[7] John Bernal, a British science historian, writes in *Science in History* (1954) that "Movable metal types were first used by Koreans in the fourteenth century [note: in fact the thirteenth century]. It was introduced into Europe in the mid-fifteenth century and spread extraordinarily rapidly."

30. Armored Cavalry of Koguryo

The kingdom of Koguryo, one of Korea's Three Kingdoms, overcame several large-scale Chinese invasions, and was a formidable military power. The iron-clad rider and horse – or *kaema* warrior – enabled Koguryo forces to break an opposing line of enemy soldiers, and led to many victories over large armies with comparatively small numbers. The *kaema* were the first full armored cavalry troops. The advanced steelmaking techniques of Koguryo – enabling mass production of high quality steel – were behind this. This tradition is being continued in the 21st century, with the Korean steelmaker POSCO developing a new process of steel production to replace the blast furnace.

Koguryo (BC 37~AD 668) was one of the Three Kingdoms of ancient Korea, together with Paekche and Silla. Ever since it was founded near a tributary of the Amrok river two millennia ago, it occupied the northern part of the Korean peninsula and much of southern Manchuria, and was a powerful nation in East Asia.

According to *The Book of Sui*, an official history of the Chinese Sui dynasty, China launched four campaigns against Koguryo within 16 years. The army assembled for the second campaign in 612 AD was a vast force of 3.3 million, of which roughly one third were combat troops and the rest support. *The Book of Sui* records that, with one battalion of Sui forces departing each day, it took 40 days for all the companies to depart, and the length of the army stretched some 377 km (230 miles). An expedition of this size would not be undertaken again until the 18th century.

In the war that ensued, the Koguryo Prince Konmu's 500 warriors defeated

Kaema warriors depicted in the Koguryo mural paintings (4~5th century AD)

the Sui Navy at the Castle of Pyongyang, Koguryo's capital, and General Ulji Mundok destroyed the majority of the retreating Sui forces at the Battle of Salsu. Sui resumed its attempted conquest of Koguryo in 613 and 614, but these campaigns also ended in failure, and eventually led to the fall of the Sui dynasty itself.

The *kaema musa*, or armored cavalry, enabled Koguryo to maintain the upper hand in this war with the Sui and hold considerable influence in East Asia over a long period of time. Both the warrior and his horse were fully clad in steel armor, and the rider held a spear longer than 5.4m mounted upon his shoulders. When the warrior charged, the momentum of the horse at full gallop and the weight of the armor invariably broke the ranks of the opposing infantry. With superior armor and offensive power, the main purpose of the *kaema* warrior was to penetrate the enemy lines and disrupt their formation. In terms of modern warfare, they performed a role similar to that of a tank.

The *kaema* warriors are often depicted in Koguryo mural paintings, and appear for the first time in literature in the *History of Three Kingdoms*. This recounts how King Tongchon (r. 227~248) repelled an invasion by the Chinese Wei dynasty with a force of twenty thousand men, which included 5,000 *kaema* warriors.

The sheer scale of the five thousand *kaema* warriors mobilized for the occasion can be appreciated from the amount of steel that would have been needed for their equipment. Assuming that 40kg of steel was needed to outfit the horse, 20kg for the warrior's armor and 10kg for his weapons, a total of 70kg of steel was required for every *kaema* warrior. To arm five thousand, 350 tons of steel would have been needed. If we factor in a reserve amount, this comes to 500 tons. Almost 1,800 years ago, it would have been a tremendous undertaking to produce such an enormous amount of steel.

Horse armor has been discovered in the hills near the Euphrates, and as a result the origin of the armored horse and rider is generally traced back to

Steel armor for a horse, excavated in Haman, South Kyongsang Province

Ancient Greek civilization. Given that the area was developed around the 4th century BC and destroyed by the Persians in 256 AD, we can infer that armored cavalry appeared before the 3rd century AD. However, the cavalry armor covered only the front-half of the horse. Similar armor was also used by the Scythians, a powerful horse-riding tribe, from the 3rd~2nd century BC, as well as by the neighboring nations of Armenia, Parthia, and Persia, although they too did not cover the entire body of the horse with steel armor.

There are various reasons why heavy cavalry were not used more extensively. In the first place, the cost of harnessing both the horse and the troops in full steel armor was very high. The English scholar John Warry estimates that the cost of purchasing a single suit of armor for a heavy infantryman (hoplite) in Ancient Greece would have been equivalent to the purchase of a car today, while the outlay would have been three or four times greater for heavy cavalry. A more fundamental reason, however, for the rareness of heavy cavalry is the need for advanced steelmaking. Koguryo had inherited advanced steelmaking techniques from the Old Choson period, and because Manchuria possessed a good supply of high-quality iron ore, they were able to deploy their heavy cavalry more freely.

Old Choson possessed unique expertise in the field of steel-making, which was passed on to subsequent generations. This is how Koguryo, a successor to Old Choson, was able to produce high-grade steel and equip every cavalryman and horse with steel weapons and armor. In testimony to the sophisticated technology of Old Choson, a round mirror made of iron has been excavated from a tomb in Pyongyang, measuring 15 cm in diameter and 0.5 cm in thickness. Its absolute age goes back to 12th century BC, making it the oldest surviving iron artifact in East Asia. This iron-mirror was made not through a process of beating, but was cast from fully molten iron obtained directly from the smelting furnace.

An iron broach excavated from another district in Pyongyang, made with 7th century tool-steel, has kept its form intact with a full range of chisel indentations visible along its length. It contains 1% carbon, 0.15% silicon, 0.0007% sulfur, and registers 426HB on the Brinell scale. There is no evidence of welding on the broach, and its structural composition is one that could only have been formed at a high temperature. Modern scientists are amazed by these two artifacts, as they were clearly made with iron reduced to a completely molten state, for the first time in East Asia.

The advanced steel technology of the ancient kingdoms of Korea lives on in 21st century Korea. Korea's leading steel producer POSCO has successfully developed and tested FINEX, the next-generation steelmaking technology that is set to replace the blast furnace, beginning a new chapter in the history of steelmaking.

The traditional blast furnace has been favored for its high productivity, potential for large-scale production, and high quality output. As part of the worldwide efforts to overcome environmental issues in the steel making process, and also in view of rising raw material prices, POSCO developed a new process called FINEX. Through eliminating the preliminary processes of coking and sintering, as well as operating with low-grade, low-cost ore fines and coal, the capital and operating costs for a next-generation FINEX plant are approximately 20% and 15% lower respectively, without compromising the rate and quality of production. Pollution is also significantly decreased, with pollutants such as sulfur oxides (SOx) and nitrogen oxides (NOx) reduced to only 1-3% of current levels. As such, FINEX is expected to revolutionize the steelmaking industry.

31. First Use of Naval Artillery

The first naval artillery battle took place in Korea in 1380, 200 years before the Battle of Lepanto in the West. Naval artillery methods were developed by the Korean inventor Choi Mu-son in response to the large-scale incursions of Japanese pirates. Korean military science had foundered during an extended period of peace, but with persistence, Choi Mu-son re-discovered how to make gunpowder, and invented a range of naval weapons, which enabled Korea to break the power of the Japanese pirate navy in three major naval engagements.

In military history, the use of artillery at sea marked the beginning of modern naval warfare. It is for this reason that the Battle of Lepanto (1571), in which the allied forces of Venice, Genoa, and Spain overcame the Turks by superior numbers of cannons, is viewed as a turning point in water-borne combat. In the aftermath of Lepanto, countries with formidable naval firepower such as Spain, Portugal, England, and the Netherlands, gained control of the sea, and came to play a leading role in world history.

Some 200 years before the Battle of Lepanto, the world's first naval artillery battle took place off the coast of Korea. In the Battle of Chinpo (1380), 80 Koryo warships, equipped with firearms invented by Choi Mu-son, sank 500 Japanese *wako*, or pirate ships.

Development of Naval Artillery

Towards the end of the Koryo period (918~1392), the Japanese *wako* represented Korea's biggest threat. During the reign of King Wu alone (r. 1374~1388), 378 *wako* coastline attacks were recorded within 14 years. The *wako* were a large and well-orchestrated operation, with 200-500 ships used in any given raid. Initially, they were able to come and go as they pleased, raiding houses and taking food, property, and lives.

The reason for the sudden increase in Japanese piracy during this period was the internal conflict in Japan that spanned the 70 years between 1322 and 1392. The country was divided into north and south[8], and as the authority of the central government did not extend to the provinces, the local clans took the opportunity to form piracy operations in order to acquire food and wealth, and engaged in the systematic looting of neighboring countries.

At the time, there were two main methods of naval attack. The first technique was to pierce the sides of an enemy vessel by means of a pointed ram fixed near the bow below the waterline. This was an ancient strategy, going back to the days of Greece and Rome, and a favored naval tactic in the West, used until the Battle of Trafalgar in the early 19th century.

The other technique was to 'grapple and board.' As the name suggests, the enemy vessel drew alongside, boarded the ship, and attempted to take it over by means of hand-to-hand combat. The Romans overcame the Carthaginian navy with this method, and it was also commonly used by pirates, including the *wako* in their invasions of Korea. Since they were skilled in this kind of 'melee' combat, they placed great emphasis on swift approach and boarding.

In response, Korea chose to engage the pirates on land, allowing them to come aground and laying ambushes for them. As the *wako* pillaging continued, almost the entire coastline became uninhabitable, and Korea began to attempt to repel the Japanese pirates by sea. This campaign was made possible by the discoveries of an eminent scientist and inventor named Choi Mu-son. The son of

---

[8] Although there was one emperor, the two contending courts of North and South alternated on the throne by agreement.

an official in the local government, he was born in 1325 in Yongju, Kyongsang Province. He investigated ways to defeat the *wako* vessels without coming into direct contact with them, and thus running the risk being boarded. His investigations led to the development of naval cannons and gunpowder-based naval artillery, which had never been used before anywhere in the world.

It is well known that gunpowder was invented in China, and in Korea too, gunpowder firearms were manufactured and deployed from an early stage. According to the *Sejo Sillok*, gunpowder cannons were first made in the Kingdom of Silla (BC 57~AD 935), and underwent a period of refinement during the Koryo period (918~1392). Their development was halted, however, by changes in the political climate. As foreign invasions declined, and the power of civil officials grew, during the closing years of the Koryo period the military profession became less esteemed, and as a result, the Department of Arms Manufacture was decommissioned in 1308, and the military training grounds were shut in 1343. Towards the end of the 14th century, when *wako* piracy was at its height, Korea had long forgotten how to make gunpowder.

Initially, Korea requested gunpowder from China. China was unable to refuse Korea's request outright, as they were allies against Japan, but did not wish to give them the full amount. On various pretexts, China sent far less than what was required, and in the end, the Royal Court of Koryo was compelled to produce gunpowder for itself. It was by now a matter of national urgency, and Choi was placed in charge. Gunpowder at the time was the equivalent of nuclear weapons today, and nations guarded their methods of manufacture with great secrecy. Therefore Korea had little choice but to devise and build its own independent manufacturing facilities.

Choi first examined available historical records containing information about how gunpowder had been made in the past. He was able to establish that it involved mixing sulfur with willow charcoal and saltpeter. Sulfur and charcoal were readily available, but he was initially unable to determine how saltpeter had been made. After countless trials and many failed attempts, Choi finally determined a basic method for making gunpowder.

In order to mass-produce it, however, he needed to devise a more straightforward method. He therefore visited the Pyokran Island,[9] a place often frequented by foreigners, and inquired after people who might be able to reveal the secret to him. Eventually he came across a Chinese technician called Yi Won, and learnt from him the details of an efficient manufacturing process. With this, Choi was able to produce gunpowder consisting of 75% potassium nitrate, 10% sulfur, and 15% charcoal, identical in composition to modern black gunpowder.

Choi then proceeded to design gunpowder-based weapons, such as the *hwajon* ('fire arrow') and the *hwatong* ('fire barrel'). After successful trial runs, he recommended that the Royal Court set up a new government office to oversee the production of gunpowder and various gunpowder-based weapons. His proposal was accepted, and in 1377 the Office of Heavy Artillery was set up with Choi as the head. Here he developed 18 different varieties of firearm.

The World's First Naval Artillery Battle

In 1380, *wako* pirates raided the Korean port of Chinpo with a huge force of 500 warships. The crew capacity of the ships is said to have been 25 for the smallest vessels, 50 for medium-sized vessels, and 100 for the largest. Even if we assume the majority were small or medium-sized vessels, the total number of troops would have been close to 25,000. According to the *Overview of Koryo History* (1452), the pirates left piles of rice in the fields 15 cm high, spilled in the course of their pillaging. Although this perhaps contains an element of

---

[9] A maritime hub in the Koryo period, the island was situated in the lower section of Yesong River near the capital Kaesong.

exaggeration, it gives an idea of the scale of the looting.

On hearing the news of the *wako* attack, the Royal Court immediately dispatched 80 warships under the command of Na Se. Against the *wako* fleet of five hundred, 80 seemed a paltry figure, but when they arrived at Chinpo and began the counter-offensive, the battle was over very quickly. Koryo's naval artillery caused devastating damage to the enemy ships, setting the fleet ablaze within moments. Such was Battle of Chinpo (1380), the world's first naval battle settled by means of gunpowder-based artillery.

In 1383, three years after the Battle of Chinpo, the *wako* invaded the southern coast with a fleet of 120 ships to avenge their defeat. The Korean Admiral Chong Chi attacked with 47 warships armed with heavy artillery, and in the battle near the port of Kwanumpo burned 17 enemy vessels and overcame 2,400 pirates. In the aftermath of this victory, Koryo adopted a more proactive approach to fighting piracy, and decided to attack Tsushima Island, the heart of *wako* operations. In 1389, Commander Park Wi set sail for the Island with a fleet of 100 vessels. The campaign was a resounding success. Park's navy sank 300 pirate ships lying in anchor along the island's shores, and rescued 100 Korean citizens held there as hostages.

After the Koryo navy had completely suppressed the *wako* pirates using heavy artillery in the Battle of Chinpo, the Battle of Kwanumpo, and the expedition to Tsushima Island, diplomatic relations between Koryo and Japan began to thaw. Since 1375, Koryo had sent envoys to Japan on an almost annual basis, requesting them to restrain the *wako* attacks. The Royal Court of Japan generally responded with indifference, stating that it was beyond the power of a central government to control the activities of pirates.

In the 1380s, as Koryo's campaign against the *wako* proved successful, Japan began to show greater interest in pursuing an amicable relationship, frequently sending emissaries to offer tribute and return captives. It is likely that the newly-revealed power of Koryo's naval artillery influenced this change of attitude.

32. Koryo Shipbuilding

Naval artillery can only be used if the standard of shipbuilding is advanced enough to compensate for the weight and recoil of the firearm. The level of Koryo's shipbuilding was remarkably high, as attested by records of campaigns in which they fought alongside other vessels. Not only were the ships well-structured and capable of heavy loads, Koryo shipbuilders were able to build them at a startling rate – as many as 75 per month. When we consider that the standard size and rate of production even later in world history was far below this, these achievements are truly astonishing.

Once artillery weapons have been designed and built, one might think that all that remains is to put them on board a ship. However, installing a heavy firearm on a vessel is not straightforward. When the artillery is used, it subjects the ship to a huge recoil. Since ships were made of wood, if its displacement was sufficiently small, a ship could capsize as a result. Even if it does not roll over, the jolt can impair the accuracy of the firearms and affect the vessel's stability.

Choi's heavy artillery was able to fulfill its potential only because Koryo's shipbuilding was of a sufficient standard to support it fully. The standard of Koryo's warships was put to the test when, under compulsion from the Mongolian Yuan dynasty, they set sail with Yuan forces for a campaign against Japan in 1268. In an account of this naval campaign, the Chinese *History of Yuan* gives the following account, "We ran into a storm, and due to the high waves, our warships collided with one another and most were destroyed. Only the warships of Koryo could sail on, and having successfully carried out their mission they returned home."

Prior to this campaign, Yuan had requested 300 vessels from Koryo, each capable of transporting 3,000~4,000 sacks of military provisions, weighing roughly 240~320 tons. The weight of each vessel in terms of total carriage must therefore have been 400~500 tons. Koryo managed to build 300 such ships in four months.

In order to understand the scale of this achievement, it may help to examine it in the light of Christopher Columbus' expedition to the New World in 1492, 200 years later.

Columbus' discovery of America was made possible by the patronage of Ferdinand II and Isabella I of Spain. The patron to whom Columbus had initially turned for support, however, was John II of Portugal. In 1484, Columbus presented the details of his expedition to the Portuguese monarch, and requested John II to provide caravels for his expedition to investigate routes to India. The caravel was a ship developed by Infante Henrique of Portugal (Prince Henry the Navigator), and was the most sophisticated vessel of its day, incorporating every development in shipbuilding since the days of the Mediterranean galleys. It was typically 50 tons or more, and its deep hull allowed for a large load of cargo. With its numerous masts, huge triangular staysail and square-rig, the ship was more than 30 meters long and over 12 meters wide.

Believing that the wealth of India would be his when the western sea-route was found, John II initially favored the proposal, and commissioned a study on the feasibility of the voyage, principally to determine whether a journey to India would be possible with the caravels that Columbus had requested. The study was undertaken by Toscanelli, the celebrated mathematician of Florence. Toscanelli estimated the circumference of the Earth to be 39,400km (only 675km short of the actual 40,075km), and on this basis he assessed the feasibility of Columbus' plan. Given Portugal's naval capabilities, he concluded that the plan was impossible. The primary obstacle was the carrying capacity of the caravel, which was too small to carry sufficient provisions for a long journey to India.

Toscanelli added that the plan might be possible if provisions could be replenished en-route (i.e. making frequent stops at islands). This was in fact how Columbus eventually succeeded, but at the time there was no guarantee that such islands would appear.

Learning the conclusions of Toscanelli's report, the Portugese monarch rejected Columbus' proposal. It was not until Columbus had secured the support of the Spanish court that he was finally able to set sail. On the evening of August 3, 1492, Columbus departed from the Spanish port of Palos de la Frontera with the *Santa María*, *Pinta* and *Niña*, and a crew of 120 sailors. To discover a new route to India, the longest voyage ever attempted at the time, Columbus left with the largest ships then available. The flagship *Santa Maria* was 150 tons, and the *Pinta* and *Niña*, 60 and 50 tons respectively.

Viewed in this context, it is easier to appreciate the achievement of the Koryo shipbuilders, who in 1268 succeeded in building three hundred ships weighing 400~500 tons in four months.

33. *Singijeon*: 15th Century Rocket Artillery

There are records of gunpowder being used in Korea as early as the 7th century AD. Choi Mu-son, the inventor of naval artillery, developed 18 different firearms, including a self-propelled arrow called *chuhwa*, which later in the 15th century became a rocket called *singijeon* that detonated upon impact, and won Korea key victories in the war against the invading Japanese. Essentially a two-stage rocket, the *singijeon* came in three sizes. The biggest was 5.3m long, and until the mid-19th century was the world's largest rocket.

Gunpowder-based weapons were in use in Korea much earlier than is commonly believed. *Prerequisites for a Military Commander*, a war manual published in the latter half of the Choson period (1392~1910), explains the principles of explosives, and gives an account of ancient gunpowder-based weapons called *chung-jon-roe* and *hwa-roe-po*. Academics have assigned these weapons to the Three Kingdoms period (57 BC~ AD 668). In the *History of the Three Kingdoms,* also, the army of Silla is said to have used 'black powder' against Koguryo in the battle of Pukhansan Castle in 661.[10]

During the Koryo dynasty (918~1392), because wars with the nomadic tribes of Kitans, Jurchens, Mongols, and the *wako* pirates were so frequent, many new weapons were developed. Gunpowder and related artillery technology took huge strides forward to ensure Korea's security. This development started again at the close of the 14th century, when gunpowder-based weapons emerged as a means

---

[10] Gunpowder is known to have been developed in China in the 8th century. However, based on the battle of Pukhansan Castle, certain scholars maintain that saltpeter firearms were invented in Korea one century earlier.

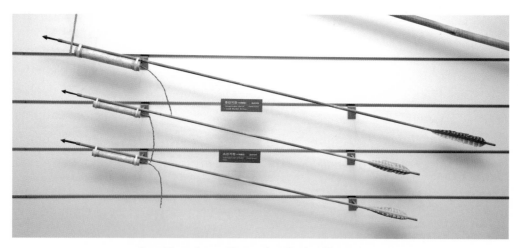

Small and medium sized *singijeon*

of repelling the resurgent *wako* pirates who were ravaging the nation.

Of the 18 different kinds of gunpowder-based firearm developed by Choi Mu-son, there was one called *chuhwa*, which literally means 'a running fire.' It was a jet-propelled arrow based on the same principle as modern day rockets. The *chuhwa* continued to be developed during the new Choson dynasty, and in the 15th century was reborn as a powerful rocket called *singijeon*. Unlike the other firearms of the day, it produced a deafening noise in flight, discharging much fire and smoke. Detonating automatically upon reaching its target, it struck terror into the hearts of the enemy. New weapons such as *singijeon* played a pivotal role in the Battle of Haengju, one of the three great battles of the Imjin War (1592~1598), in which 2,800 Koreans emerged victorious against a 30,000-strong Japanese army.

The *singijeon* consisted of an arrow, which formed the body of the rocket, an ignition-barrel carrying the explosive, and a fuel-barrel containing the rocket propellant. The ignition barrel and fuel-barrel were attached to the arrow, and when it was fired, it was propelled firstly by the fuel-barrel propellant, and then by the ignition-barrel, much like a two-stage rocket. The rocket would explode when it reached the enemy target up to 1000m away.

Singijeon were made in large, medium, and small sizes. The largest variety was the *tae-singijeon*, an enormous rocket measuring 5.3 meters in length. Propelled by the fuel-barrel (69.5 cm long, 95.5 cm in diameter), the explosive located inside in the ignition-barrel (22.8 cm long, 7.46 cm in diameter) detonated on impact to neutralize the enemy. The *singijeon* was larger than the 32-pound rocket developed by Sir William Congreve in 1806 (4.6m long), and rockets on a scale comparable to the *singijeon* would not appear until the latter half of the 19th century. For more than 300 years since its development in 1448, the *singijeon* was the world's largest and most powerful rocket.

Ironically, the technical details of the *singijeon* were unknown until very recently. Although Korean historians knew of the design, as it was included as an appendix of *Kukjo Orye Sorye* (1474), it was not realized what device the design referred to until 1975, when Chae Yeon-suk, former president of the Korea Aerospace Research Institute, confirmed that they were the lost plans of the *singijeon*. The appendix gives details of the lengths of the wooden materials used to the nearest 0.3 mm, and is one of the most striking pieces of evidence for the advanced science of 15th century Korea.

34. *Hwacha*: Mobile Multi-Rocket Launcher

The *Hwacha* launcher was capable of firing 100 s*ingijeon* rockets at a time. The moveable platform on which the *Hwacha* was mounted was easy to maneuver, and the platform was positioned above the wheels in order to enable a greater elevation of fire. Originally developed by the son of Choi Mu-son, it was later improved to include defensive features under King Munjong, and continued to improve throughout the Choson period, incorporating features such as the ability to rotate 360 degrees, and to fire other projectiles such as cannon balls.

The power of the 15th century s*ingijeon* rocket was taken to a new level by the *Hwacha* launcher, a radical device which could fire 100 s*ingijeon* rockets in a single volley. According to *Kukjo Orye Sorye* (1474), the launcher consisted of 100 rectangular prisms arranged in seven rows. The prisms were 56 mm wide and 234 mm long, and each contained a cylindrical hole 47 mm in diameter. Each of these 100 holes was loaded with a medium or small-sized s*ingijeon*. By connecting together the fuses of the s*ingijeon*, the *Hwacha* launcher was capable of firing its entire load of projectiles with a single ignition, a truly revolutionary system at the time.

The first *Hwacha* was built by Choi Hae-son, the son of Choi Mu-son, but an improved and more robust version was later developed by King Munjong in 1451. The distinctive feature of the *Munjong Hwacha,* as documented in the annals, was that shields were installed on either side to protect the gunner, and steel plates were built into the launch pad of the s*ingijeon*, as a precaution against the risk of fire.

The moveable platform used to transport the *Hwacha* had a unique structure.

Normally, a platform is positioned immediately above the wheel-axis, but in the *Munjong Hwacha,* it was higher than the wheels (see picture). This was to enable a more elevated angle of fire. The *Hwacha* could be angled at 45 degrees, the ideal angle for gunpowder-based weapons[11].

The *Hwacha* platform had only two wheels, and since it was not very large, it benefited from greater mobility. According to the *Sillok* (Royal Annals), it could be moved easily on level ground by just two people, and four people could maneuver it across any type of terrain. It was thus the world's first mobile launcher vehicle.

Hwacha was especially useful in breaking up enemy formations and siege lines. In 1492, it played an integral role in repelling an invasion from the North. Its full potential was demonstrated during the Imjin War (1592~1598) when General Kwon Yul is said to have deployed 300 *Hwacha* launchers in his defense of the Haengju Fortress.

The *Hwacha* continued to evolve, and the *Kosa Sinso*, published in 1771, gives an account of a more developed version of the launcher vehicle. Built with pine boards and shaped like a large crate, swords thrust out from the inside when the vehicle was in motion, and retracted when it was stationary. This version of *Hwacha* had a three-wheeled platform, and fired both cannon balls and bombs. Thanks to a specially designed pivot-point, the cannon was able to turn freely in all directions. The gun barrel could therefore rotate 360 degrees like a tank, and could also be fixed at a certain angle of elevation in order to give greater control over the missile's trajectory.

---

[11] When the angle is increased from 20 to 40 degrees, for example, the projectile travels 1.5 times further.

Replica of *Hwacha* The War Memorial of Korea

35. The World's First Time Bomb

Launched into enemy camps and formations using the *Wangu* mortar, the *Pigyok Chincholloe* was the world's first timed explosive device. It was developed by Yi Chang-son during the Imjin War of the 16th century, and used to great effect by the Choson commanders. The bombs inflicted both damage and terror upon the enemy, who assumed that supernatural forces were at work. The timing device was a bamboo cylinder, with the fuse wound in spiral fashion, the length of the fuse determining the delay to explosion.

Invented by the artillery technician Yi Chang-son during the Imjin War (1592~1598), the *Pigyok Chincholloe* (literally meaning 'shaking the heavens with lightning and thunder') was the world's first time bomb. In *Precautions for the Future*, written by the Prime Minister Ryu Song-yong in the war's aftermath, there is a detailed account of how Kyongju Castle was recaptured using the bomb.

With 10,000 soldiers from the Left Province Army, General Park Chin advanced until he reached the gate of Kyongju Castle. The enemy, however, secretly exited by the North Gate, and launched a surprise assault from the rear. The general had no option but to withdraw to the River An. On the same night, Park Chin again advanced to the castle, and hiding his troops near the castle gate, he fired *Pigyok Chincholloe* within the walls. The bomb landed on the ground in front of the enemy tent, and not knowing what it was, the enemy soldiers pressed forward in order to gain a closer look. Some moments later, the bomb exploded. There was a huge sound as the explosion shook the earth, and metal shrapnel scattered in all directions. 30 were killed instantly, and many collapsed with shock. When the survivors came back to their senses, still unable understand how it had been done, they claimed it was the doing of evil spirits. On the following morning, the enemy abandoned the castle and fled to the port of Sosaeng.

In the August of the following year, Japanese forces laid siege to the castle once more, but were again unable to withstand the firepower of the *Pigyok Chincholloe*, and retreated. *The Implements of War*, published in Japan, documented the power of the bomb.

> During the Imjin War, cannons were used extensively by the Korean army, who poured explosives upon us and inflicted great damage. At the time, our army had only just become acquainted with cannons, and we could not match the enemy.

Here, 'explosives' refers to the *Pigyok Chincholloe* and 'cannons' to the *Wangu* mortar. The *Pigyok Chincholloe* was fired using the *Tae-Wangu*, the largest class of mortar, recorded by the *Choson Sillok* as having a range of 500~600 paces. It also fired other types of projectiles, such as rocks or metal balls, and was used to destroy castle walls or attack an enemy stationed behind a barrier.

Spherical in shape and weighing about 12kg, the *Pigyok Chincholloe* was cast using pig iron, and gunpowder and metal shrapnel were placed inside. The ignition device differed from regular explosives. It consisted of a bamboo cylinder with grooves carved in a spiral fashion, and the detonating fuse wound around the indentations. The time-delay before detonation was determined by the length of the fuse: the fuse was wound 10 times for a swift explosion, and 15

 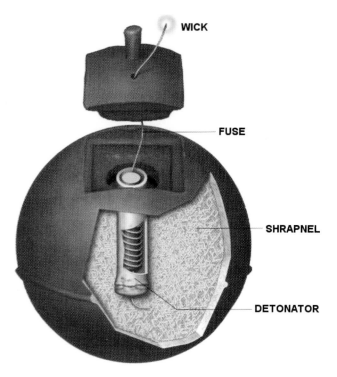

WICK

FUSE

SHRAPNEL

DETONATOR

(Left) *Pigyok Chincholloe,* 16th century, The War Meomorial of Korea

(Right) Diagram of the *Pigyok Chincholloe*

times if a longer delay was required. *Pigyok Chincholloe* is currently on display at several museums including the Yonsei University Museum, Jinju National Museum, and The War Memorial of Korea.

36. *Kobukson* or 'Turtle Ship'

Clad with iron, the 'Turtle Ship' won many sea battles against large numbers of enemy ships by means of superior fire-power and structural design. The roof was covered with iron spikes to prevent the enemy from boarding. Cannons were placed at every angle on the ship, and the 'dragon's head' emitted smoke to provide cover and distraction. The ship was well-suited for ramming, as it was sturdier than the enemy ships thanks to the red pine timber and the use of wooden nails which expanded as they absorbed seawater. The enhanced structural integrity also enabled it to carry heavier cannons than the enemy, with greater range. As with other Korean traditions, innovation on the sea has carried through to the modern age, with Korean shipbuilders currently leading the world market, both in construction of vessels and also naval constructions such as floating and 'on ground' docks.

The *Kobukson*, or Turtle Ship, was the world's first iron-armored warship. It was completed and used for the first time by Admiral Yi Sun-sin in the 16th century. With its exceptional capabilities and fire power, it played an active role in almost all the sea battles of the Imjin War (1592~1598). Able to charge and break up the enemy fleet's formation, sinking ships within minutes, the *Kobukson* was effectively a sea tank.

The bow of the *Kobukson* was shaped like the head of a dragon, and the stern was like a turtle's tail. The interior of the ship consisted of three floors: the lower floor was used to store cargo, the middle floor kept the rowers, and the top floor was the gun deck. The ship was designed so that the crew were able to see outside whilst being invisible to the enemy.

Replica of the *Kobukson* The War Memorial of Korea

Iron armor plating covered the wooden boards which roofed over the *Kobukson*. Steel spikes were then fixed in the roof, and straw laid over the top. When the enemy tried to board the ship, they were impaled on the hidden spikes.

Unlike other warships, the *Kobukson* had guns stationed not only along its sides, but also in the bow and in the stern, allowing it unprecedented flexibility of range and accuracy. The dragon's head was designed to 'exhale' flaming arrows and cannon balls, and also sulfurous fumes and clouds of smoke, which provided the Korean Navy with cover for tactical maneuvers.

A little below the bow protruded the head of a gargoyle, which served as a charging device, and was used in conjunction with the dragon head in the *Kobukson*'s special ramming technique. When the gargoyle's head breached an enemy hull, the dragon's head would fire cannon balls into the breach as the ship withdrew. The gargoyle had the further effect of improving the ship's hydrodynamic performance by cutting the waves as the ship sped along, thus increasing its ramming speed.

Two further features of the *Kobukson* made it particularly serviceable for the execution of this tactic. First, it was built with red pine timbers, which have a relative density of 0.73, much higher than that of average timber (0.41-0.47). Second, wooden nails were used in the construction of the *Kobukson*. Unlike metal nails, which are quick to rust, the wooden nails expanded as they absorbed water, and the joints became more secure over time. The *Kobukson* as a whole was constructed on this principle of strengthening by expansion: support beams were fitted to the roof by means of a system of matching indentations and interlocking teeth, thus making the entire structure of the vessel stronger and more resilient.

The Japanese ships, made out of wood with a lower density, were light and swift, but the wood was less able to withstand the recoil of cannons, and this put a restriction on the number of heavy fire-arms that could be carried on one ship. Consequently the Japanese normally preferred to use muskets, which had a maximum range of 200 meters. *Kobuksons*, on the other hand, were able to carry a whole range of different cannons on board, including long-distance cannons such as *Chon* (Heaven), with a range of over 500 meters, *Chi* (Earth), its slightly smaller companion, with a range of 350 meters, and *Seung* (Victory), a portable cannon with a range of up to 200 meters.

Replicas of *Kobukson* are on display at various national museums, such as the War Memorial of Korea, as well as other museums throughout the world, such as the Washington D.C. War Memorial Museum in North America, and in many other countries including China, Japan, Germany, France, and Canada.

With a history of innovation on the sea, Koreans are now at the forefront of the world's shipbuilding industry in the 21st century. According to a report released in February 2006 by Clarkson Research Studies, Korean shipbuilders filled the top seven places in a list of world shipbuilding companies ranked by orders and backorders. These seven Korean companies appear to have taken as much as 35% of the world market, and over 70% of the high value-added ships market, or ships which use cutting edge technology, such as 10,000 TEU class super-sized container ships, Floating Production Storage and Offloading (FPSO) vessels, and LNG carriers.

In August of 2005, New Orleans was devastated by hurricane Katrina. However, the city was able to receive the energy it needed to recover, thanks to a ship called LNG-RV (Regasification Vessel) made by the Korean company Daewoo Shipbuilding. Unlike ordinary LNG ships, which transport gas in liquid form, Daewoo's LNG-RV ship was installed with equipment that converted the liquid to gas directly on the ship, meaning that it was ready for use without the need for a working gas infrastructure onshore.

Several years ago, Samsung Heavy Industries developed the world's first forward-and-reverse directional icebreaker, for use in the Polar Regions. The vessel made it possible to break a path through the ice which covers the North Pole region whilst transporting cargo at the same time, rather than using two separate ships. Even in extreme situations, such as temperatures below 45°C, it was capable not only of cutting through a field of ice 1.57 meters deep, but also able to turn 360 degrees.

Korea's small territory, with limited natural resources, spurs on the creative spirit of its people. Korean shipbuilding companies can build ships on the water,

A vessel built on land by Hyundai Heavy Industries

without the need for dry docks. At one point, under pressure from excessive demand, Samsung Heavy Industries ran out of dock space. After careful planning, it developed the world's first large-scale 'floating dock'. The huge building blocks of the ship were assembled on the surface of a special barge, and when the ship was completely built, the barge was sunk so that the ship was left floating. The 'floating dock' method enabled Samsung to overcome the problems of side-to-side motion that normally inhibit the process of welding at sea.

Hyundai Heavy Industries, the world's largest shipbuilder, launches a new ship approximately every five days – some with 15 levels and stretching the length of three football fields. Hyundai Heavy Industries was the first to build a vessel on land, which it claimed was a breakthrough. This 'on ground building' method frees ships from the tights constraints of a dry dock, allowing them to be built in bigger sections at a time. After the ship is completed it is transported by rail and put out to sea on a barge. If development of innovative technologies such as this continues, the Korean shipbuilding industry is likely to keep its lead in the world.

37. *Chugugi* : The World's First Rain Gauge

Chugugi, completed in 1442, was the world's first rain gauge, and has yet to be improved upon by modern science. It allowed precise measurements of rainfall to be taken all around the country over a period of 400 years. The Confucian values of Korea encouraged an understanding of nature, but the rain gauge was also useful for agricultural purposes. The invention of the *Chugugi* came to be ascribed erroneously to China, owing to the use of the Chinese dating system in the inscription on a surviving model. Although the historical texts of China and Korea show it was a Korean invention, this is not currently recognized in modern textbooks that mention the rain gauge.

On 18 August 1441, a new system of rain measurement was invented in Korea, marking a turning point in the history of meteorology. Conceived by Sejong's eldest son Munjong, and developed in collaboration with other scientists, the world's first rain gauge has yet to be superseded by modern scientific instruments.

Trials of the rain gauge, made in 1441, revealed a number of shortcomings with the prototype. These were corrected, and the design was finalized on May 8th of the following year. The recalibrated rain gauge (31.9 cm in height, 14.9 cm in diameter) was given the official title *'Chugugi.'* It was distributed to the local authorities throughout the country, together with a manual for its use and manufacture. The technical specifications of the 1442 rain gauge were as follows:

(1) The rain gauge called '*Chugugi*' is made of iron.

(2) Its height is 1 *cha* 5 *chi* [31.9 cm], and its diameter 7 *chi* [14.9 cm].

(3) Measurements are taken when the rain has stopped.

(4) The *chuchok* ruler measures the water level.

(5) The date and time of rainfall must be recorded, with details of the beginning and end times.

(6) The water level must be measured accurately in *cha* (303 mm), *chi* (30.3 mm) and *pun* (3.03 mm).

The recorded rainfall was then reported in a prescribed manner, giving details of the month, location, time of day and type of rain[12]. The level of water was also recorded in a prescribed manner. With the invention of the *Chugugi*, the scientists of King Sejong had found a way to measure natural phenomena quantitatively with scientific instrumentation. Under this established regime of rainfall measurement, meteorological data from across the country was collected for over 400 years.

Sejong's scientists made similar measurements of the wind, with a specially-designed anemometer. This worked by means of a flag-shaped cloth, which indicated the direction and the speed of the wind. In the first half of the 15th century, no other nation was monitoring weather conditions with precision and on nationwide basis.

The invention of the *Chugugi* was due in part to the Confucian ideals of the Choson dynasty, and the desire to understand the laws of nature. It was also partly an effort by the government to take a more scientific approach to agriculture.

Although the *Chugugi* was a unique concept developed by King Sejong's scientists, today the invention is erroneously ascribed to China. The rain gauges

---

[12] Rainfall was classified according to 8 categories: minor rain (미우); delicate rain (세우); light rain (소우); moderate rain (하우); damaging rain (쇄우); running rain (취우); heavy rain (대우); ferocious rain (폭우)

made during the reign of King Sejong were all lost during the Imjin War (1592~1598), and the few surviving examples are from the 18th century; this is where the confusion begins.

The world was first introduced to the *Chugugi* in 1910, when a Japanese scholar called Wada Yuji (1859~1918), realizing its importance, included the best photograph of a rain gauge he could find in a dissertation on Korean meteorological observations. He was at the time running a meteorological station in Chemulpo, Korea. Originally a physics graduate from Tokyo University and a meteorological official from Japan's Ministry of Interior, Wada Yuji had studied meteorology in France from July 1889 to March 1891. Written in French, his paper was entitled 'The Rain Gauge of 15th Century Korea,' and was sent to his academic acquaintances in France. This was how *Chugugi* came to be known in Europe.

In 1911, the paper was published in the January issue of the British scientific journal *Nature*, and in the same year an English translation appeared in the 37th issue of the *Quarterly Journal of the Royal Meteorological Society*. Although the *Chugugi* had now been brought to the world's attention, the photograph in the original dissertation was of a model from 1770. Still the most widely used picture of *Chugugi* in publications today, it bears the inscription '*Konryung Kyongin Owoljo*' (建隆庚寅五月造).

When the Chinese scholars saw the picture, they naturally assumed that the gauge was originally from China, and had then been sent to Korea. '*Konryung*' in the inscription refers to Ching dynasty, and '*Kyungin Owoljo*' means it was made in the 5th month of the year *Kyongin* (1770). Unaware that Koreans used both Korean dynasties and Chinese dynasties to refer to specific periods, the scholars concluded that the device was of Chinese origin. As a result, Chinese and Taiwanese textbooks today introduce Sejong's *Chugugi* as an invention of China, and this view is accepted by western scholars.

There is no reference to '*Chugugi*' in Chinese literature, nor any historical evidence of a similar instrument being used in China to measure rainfall. In the *Royal Annals of the Choson Dynasty*, there is a clear record of how the *Chugugi* was designed by Sejong's son Munjong in the period from May 1441 to June 1442, and how models were distributed by the government to each of the Provinces. Currently, however, the history of the *Chugugi* stands uncorrected.

A *Chugugi* model from 1770

38. An Automatic Water Clock

The *Chagyongnu* was an automated water clock made in 1434. Building on Chinese and Arabian innovations, it was powered by flowing water, and the time signals were triggered by a system of falling marbles. The purpose of the automated clock was to provide a means of time-keeping that required no human input, and was therefore reliable. The external design of the clock was also elaborate, with figures of the zodiac appearing at intervals to announce the different hours of the day.

It took exactly 23 years for Professor Nam Mun-hyon of Konkuk University to reconstruct the 15th century *Chagyongnu*, a self-striking clepsydra or water clock. Originally completed in one and a half years, the *Chagyongnu* was an invention of Chang Yong-sil by commission of King Sejong, and destroyed by fire during the Imjin War (1592~1598). On 20 November 2007, five hundred years after its invention, it was successfully rebuilt.

In terms of basic design, it combined the concept of the traditional hydraulic water-clock from China with automation technology from Arabia. In grafting together the horologic technologies of China and Arabia, Chang Yong-sil invented a system which relied on an analog-digital converter.

In a newspaper interview, Professor Nam said, "Based on the documentary records, we made exhaustive attempts to verify the authenticity of our reconstruction. In the restoration project, we called upon the assistance of 30 scholars and experts who were knowledgeable in the subject, and used the most up-to-date tools. It is clear that the technology of Early Choson, 570 years ago, was highly-advanced."

The water-clock was powered by a steady flow of water, which moved the marbles and clock figures at predetermined intervals to operate the time-signaling device. In building the automatic control system, the slightest error in the size of iron marbles would mean that time was not kept accurately.

The *Chagyongnu* was commissioned by Sejong out of concern for the time-keeping officials, who were employed continuously to keep watch and call out the hours. Commotions caused by an official's failure to keep the time properly, dozing off on a hot summer night or in the winter cold, were common in both East and West. *The Royal Annals of the Choson Dynasty* gives examples of officials in charge of water-clocks who failed to make announcements on time, and were punished or dismissed as a result. The *Sejong Sillok* records: "Because those responsible for keeping the time faced heavy retribution for their mistakes, Sejong, in his concern, ordered Chang Yong-sil to make clock figures out of wood to mark the time... and from then on no human effort was needed."

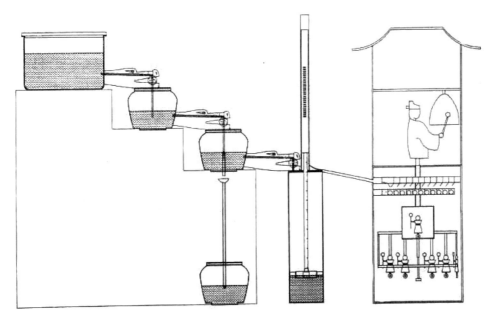

Mechanisms of *Chagyongnu* (Illustration by Nam Moon-Hyon)

After several years of research and trials, when the self striking water clock was at last complete, King Sejong ordered a pavilion to be built inside the Kyongbok Palace to house the water-clock, and held a grand banquet to celebrate the success of Chang and the other royal scientists' efforts.

Every two hours, the *Chagyongnu* would automatically ring a bell, and one of the twelve zodiac animals would appear to indicate the time.[8] The signal from the water clock would travel from the Palace to the main street of the capital city, and announced the opening and closing times of the Four Capitals Gates.

Some of the key features of *Chagyongnu* are given below, taken from Professor Nam Moon-hyon's book, *Chang Yong-sil and Chagyongnu*, published by Seoul National University Press in 2002.

(1) The Archetypal Korean Water-Clock

The inflow vessels of other East Asian water-clocks were installed with an outlet, so that excess water could be discharged when the vessel reached full capacity. Korean water-clocks worked in the same way, but had two water receiving vessels instead of one. These could be used alternately, thus avoiding delays and enabling the time to be recorded with greater accuracy.

The water clock was also built on a large scale to minimize errors of a hydrodynamic nature. Since the speed of fluid movement was linked directly to fluid temperature, the water reservoir was made as big as possible to keep the temperature at a constant level. As a result, while previous water clocks measured in units of only 15 minutes, *Chagyongnu* operated using smaller increments of time.

---

[8] In Asia, each day was divided into twelve hours, and the twelve hours were represented by twelve animals: rat, ox, tiger, rabbit, dragon, snake, horse, goat, monkey, chicken, dog, and pig.

(2) Creation of an Analog-to-Digital Conversion System

The second significant feature of the self-striking water clock lies in its signal conversion system. The 'analog' time data, displayed on the scales of the water clock's measuring rod, was converted into 'digital' data in order to signal the time automatically at specified intervals. The conversion device was called *pangmok*, and was placed above the inflow vessel that measured the time, the first device of its kind in the world. Professor Li Zhi Chao of the University of Science and Technology in China acclaimed the *pangmok*'s method of analog-to-digital conversion as one of the most important inventions in history.

(3) Creative Use of Marble-Operated Jackwork Figures

The third notable feature of the water clock is the figures operated by marbles and levers that appear to announce the time. The introduction of such mechanisms paved the way for jackworks powered by the impact of falling marbles. The small iron marbles released by the *pangmok* traveled via a copper cylinder, and dislodged marbles one by one from the reservoir loaded underneath. The copper cylinder was designed to ensure the correct sequence of release. As the small iron marbles fell from the cylinder, they pressed down upon spoon-shaped levers and dislodged the larger, egg-sized marbles. This intermediary stage served to amplify the power of the time-signaling device. The larger iron marbles then passed by a designated route to act upon the figures themselves, causing the arm to strike the bell, and the figures were displayed in succession to indicate the various hours of the day. Other figures, which struck the drum and the gong, worked on the same principle.

With its highly complex design, the water-clock's time-signaling device may be seen as equivalent to a modern-day counting machine. The figures themselves represented the pinnacle of measurement and control engineering in the early

15th century, and are among the greatest inventions in the early history of robotics and automation.

ANTIQUARIAN
HOROLOGY

AND THE PROCEEDINGS OF THE ANTIQUARIAN HOROLOGICAL SOCIETY

Illustration by Ha, Gyeong-ho, of the complete arrangement of the Automatic Striking Water Clock, or Striking Clepsydra (*chagyŏngnu*), which was constructed during the seven years (1432-1439) of astronomical undertakings for re-equipping the Korean Royal Observatory during King Sejong's reign (r. 1418-1450) of the Chosŏn dynasty (1392-1910).

The water clock was built by Chang Yŏng-shil at the command of King Sejong in September of 1433 and set up in the Annunciating Clepsydra Pavilion (Porugak) in the Kyŏngbok Palace. It was used for the first time on the first day of the eighth month of 1434 as the standard annunciator of time for the nation. (See 'Book Reviews' this issue).

NUMBER TWO   VOLUME NINETEEN   WINTER 1990

The current issue at £7·00 per copy, and available back numbers, may be obtained from the Publications Department.

The 1990 winter edition of *Antiquarian Horology*, a British publication, carried on its front cover the illustration of the Self-Striking Clepsydra by Ha Kyong-ho.

39. Jade Water Clock

The 'Jade Water Clock' was a more advanced version of the *Chagyongnu*, and displayed the different positions of the sun during the 24 solar terms. It had the practical purpose of indicating the farm work currently being undertaken throughout the kingdom, but was also a visually elaborate work of art. Made in the shape of a mountain, two series of model figures appeared to announce the hours, and the sun was represented by a gold-painted cannon ball, setting and rising according to the time of year. The scenery around the mountain changed according to the seasons. Most extraordinarily of all, everything occurred automatically, without the need for human input.

When the automated *Chagyongnu* was complete, Chang Yong-sil invented another more advanced automated clock. He wanted to design a new model combining the functions of a self-striking water clock and an astronomical armillary sphere, which would display the different positions of the sun throughout the seasons and the 24 solar terms, and allow the residents at the palace to see what work needed to be done in the rural communities during that period[14]. Chang informed King Sejong of his plan, who gladly gave his permission for the project.

Four years later, the new 'Jade Water Clock' was installed in a building

---

[14] In East Asia, 24 solar terms were used to designate the yearly changes in the weather, and were used essentially as a calendar for farmers. For example, *Ipchun* (the start of spring) fell on February 4th, when farmers began to plow the land. *Ipchu* (the start of autumn) was the time when the rice was beginning to ripen and the time for harvest was near, and so on.

adjacent to the King's chambers in the Humgyong Tower, so that he could consult it frequently. Regrettably, the clock was destroyed by fire in the Imjin War, and the plans were also lost. The description that survives in *The Royal Annals of the Choson Dynasty*, however, is truly extraordinary.

> Inside the Humgyong Tower was a mountain made out of paper 7 *chok* high (210 cm). Model clouds floated around the middle of the mountain, and the model sun rose and set according to the solar terms. Jade dolls rode upon the clouds with golden bells in their hand, shaking them at every double hour, and figures came forward with tablets bearing the time. Simultaneously, the animal corresponding to the hour would emerge from an opening in the level ground. At the foot of the mountain stood the Four Guardians in the four cardinal directions, rotating every hour. All these mechanisms moved unassisted as the clepsydra's water-wheel turned.

The golden image of the sun, made out of a cannon ball, rose and set according to the actual rising and setting times of the sun, and its inclination varied according to the polar distance. Around the mountain were paintings depicting the rural scenery of the four seasons, wood carvings of men, birds, and plants, as well as the different types of labor undertaken at different times of the year. As the seasons changed, the scenery depicted around the base of the mountain would change also, creating a truly panoramic effect.

According to the writings of the contemporary scientist Kim Ton, the automated water-clocks from other nations all required a degree of human input, whereas the Jade Clepsydra moved by itself without the need for any manual intervention. When it was made, therefore, the Jade Water Clock was one of the most sophisticated time-keeping instruments in the world.

40. The Astronomical Clock

The astronomical clock *Honchon* is known for combining Eastern and Western horological traditions. It has been praised for its own merits as a device by scholars around the world. Powered by a system of weights, the clock told the time both by means of a series of automatically displayed placards as well as with audible signals.

The *Honchon*, preserved today in the Korea University Museum, is an astronomical clock built by Song Yi-yong in 1669, and the only example of its kind in the world. Acclaimed by the British scholar Joseph Needham as "a landmark in the history of East Asian horology[15]," and requested by the Smithsonian Institution for a touring exhibition of its museums in the U.S., the clock represents the harmony of Eastern and Western horological traditions.

While the instrument is unique for its incorporation of Western-style clockwork, it is at the same time remarkably faithful to ancient East Asian horological tradition. Introduced to world academics by W. Rufus in his book *Astronomy in Korea*, written in 1930, its technical features were praised highly in *Heavenly Clockwork*, written by J. Needham, W. Ring, D. Price and others in 1960. This was followed by an in-depth analysis of the clock's mechanical principles in 1986, carried out by Needham and his colleagues in the *Hall of Heavenly Records: Korean Astronomical Instruments and Clocks 1380~1780*.

The astronomical clock principally consists of the armillary spheres and the clockwork. The armillary[16], measures around 40cm in diameter, and the

---

[15] The art of measuring time or making clocks, watches, etc.
[16] See footnote on page 33 in chapter 26: Astronomy under King Sejong.

The Astronomical Clock
Built by Song Yi-yong in 1669,
National Treasure No. 230,
Korea University Museum

terrestrial globe placed at its center is approximately 8.9cm. The armillary indicates the positions of the sun and the moon, and is similar to today's calendar.

The clockwork is powered by the motions of two weights, and is housed inside a wooden case measuring 120cm long, 52.3cm wide, and 98cm high. The higher of the two weights (weight 1 in the diagram) generates the energy that drives the clock, and corresponds to the pendulum of a grandfather clock. The energy from the weight is transmitted to the armillary sphere on the left, as well as the clock mechanisms on the right, and simultaneously powers the two devices. The hour was visibly indicated by a vertical-axis wheel linked to a disc-shaped gear. Twelve hour-placards (similar to the hour hand) were attached to the wheel, and at every hour, the appropriate placard would be displayed through a window frame. The teeth and the gears were made from brass, cut to an extreme degree of accuracy.

The other weight moved the strike-train, which operated *Honchon*'s audible time-signals. The strike-train was in turn controlled by the periodic release of 24 iron balls, which would roll down the ball-rack and cause the iron-hammer placed across the wooden casing to strike the bell. This mechanism repeated itself as the pedals of a rotating wheel raised the iron balls back to their reservoir.

Fusing together the horology of East Asia and Europe, the *Honchon* astronomical clock represents a monumental heritage in the history of clockworks. In *Science and Civilization in China*, Joseph Needham states that 'It would be an instructive thing to have a replica of this whole instrument, together with suitable historical explanation, in every great museum of the history of science and technology in the world.'

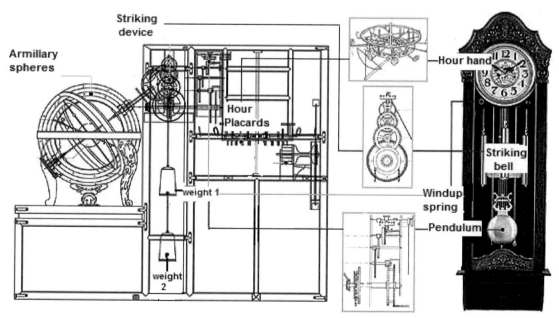

Diagram of the Astronomical Clock

41. Suwon *Hwaseong* Fortress

Hwaseong fortress, regarded by UNESCO as the epitome of military architecture, was built by Chong Yak-yong in 1796. Consisting of 48 structures, the castle complex was designed with the utmost care. As well as being beautiful to look at, the castle contains many ingenious defensive features such as the *osongji* and *chi* fortifications. Its low walls reflect the shift to artillery-based warfare, and provide overlapping fire coverage all around the perimeter. *Hwaseong* is also a site of great historical significance – King Chongjo planned the site of the new Suwon city there, and its construction was significant as the first national project undertaken with performance-based pay instead of compulsory labor. Details of the castle's design and the building process are recorded in minute detail in the *Uigwe* records, enabling the castle to be rebuilt perfectly after its destruction in the Korean War.

Entering Suwon city, the capital of Kyonggi Province, one is immediately met with the spectacle of the high Changan Gate and long fortress wall that extends in both directions. The Fortress of *Hwaseong* ('Shining Fortress') was designated as a World Heritage site in 1997 by UNESCO for its historical significance and unique architectural style.

The Epitome of East Asian Military Architecture

Suwon *Hwaseong* Fortress was completed in 1796 during the reign of King Chongjo of the Choson Dynasty. The chief architect was Chong Yak-yong, a renowned scholar official and leader of the 'practical learning' (*silhak*) movement[17]. In building the fortress, he made use of both Western and Eastern construction tools and materials, such as cranes, bricks and pulleys, and so made the fortress distinctive among the other fortresses of the East.

Hwaseong Fortress consists of 48 buildings and structures in total, including four gates that were once entrances to the old Suwon city. The fortress wall is 5.7 kilometers long and up to seven meters tall in places. The wall looks very low in comparison to the walls of other fortresses and castles, which are generally 15-20 meters tall. Why did the architects of *Hwaseong* keep the walls at such a low height?

In ancient times, the scaling of enemy castle walls was a common part of warfare. The height of the wall therefore was very important, and could determine the outcome of a battle. However, the introduction of artillery fundamentally changed this. As cannons gained importance in the battlefield, high walls became disadvantageous, for when the lower parts were damaged by artillery fire, the risk of collapse was greater.

To compensate for its low height, the architects of *Hwaseong* used large stones in order to make the wall stronger and thicker. Moreover, stone rivets measuring 1.5m in length were inserted at various places, causing the existing stones to interlock fully and so enhance the wall's structural integrity.

The Fortress was also built using an appropriate combination of stone and brick. Although stone is harder than brick, when one stone is damaged by artillery fire, the adjoining stones are also dislodged, whereas in a brick wall, the damage is limited to immediate area. The basic framework of the castle was therefore made of stone, while brick was used for the areas of greatest strategic importance, such as corners and the sections of the wall directly adjoining the castle gates.

---

[17] The *Silhak* movement opposed the strict formalism of traditional Confucianism, and the increasingly metaphysical preoccupations of its defenders, placing more emphasis the 'practical' studies of science and technology.

The Gates *Changan* (above) and *Paldal* (below)
The images on the right are from *Hwaseong Fortress Uigwe*

No two buildings in the *Hwaseong* complex are alike, and each one is beautiful to look at. This is not simply a matter of aesthetics, but the beauty of a scientific mind, which gave careful consideration to the position and purpose of each building. For example, the four main gates of *Hwaseong* are shielded by semicircular walls called *ongsung*. These served the function of a barbican, protecting the gates, the weak points in defense and the primary target in any attack. *Ongsung* made a direct assault on the gates very difficult, and even if the enemy breached its walls, they would be enclosed on all sides and vulnerable to attack.

Besides the *ongsung*, other defensive mechanisms also supplemented the castle's defenses. The Paldal Gate in the south and the Changan Gate in the north

90

Kongsimdon

Plans of *Kongsimdon* from *Hwaseong Fortress Uigwe* (1801)

are both flanked by two guard towers manned by soldiers to give an extra layer of protection. If the gate caught fire, the *osongji* came swiftly into action. An installation akin to a fire hydrant, it was installed above the gates, and poured out water from five holes linked to a water tank.

As well as being well-defended, the *Hwaseong* was also capable of powerful offensive measures, with a total of 2,700 gun embrasures, with openings in the floor so that hot water or sewage could be poured down to frustrate attempts to climb the wall.

The *Kongsimdon* is the most unusually shaped building in the fortress. Built with brick, it is circular in shape, with a spiral corridor leading to the top. Again, there are several tens of gun embrasures, stationed at various points, allowing the gunner to conceal himself easily and take aim in any direction.

Where the wall formed a straight line, defense was enhanced by *chi* installations. *Chi* is a traditional Korean fortification technique, dating back to the Koguryo period. The *chi* is a structure that protrudes from the sides of the walls, allowing soldiers to attack the enemy at different angles, and they were therefore used whenever the wall was straight.

The distance between the *chi* installations was determined by careful planning. They were placed 130 footsteps apart, and considering that the longest range of a firearm at the time was 100 footsteps, this provided a coverage overlap of 70 footsteps. Blind spots were thereby reduced, and defense was proportionately strengthened. When we map out the areas of fire coverage provided by each of the defensive facilities in *Hwaseong*, two or three overlapping layers are formed around the perimeters of the fortress, which eliminated any blind spots. Suwon *Hwaseong* was a truly impregnable complex that permitted no enemy to advance undetected or unopposed.

The International Council on Monuments and Sites (ICOMOS) states '*Hwaseong* has a unique historic significance as it was built combined with features of castle types both in Europe and in far-eastern Asia.' Nimal De Silva, who conducted the field inspection by UNESCO, observed that although *Hwaseong* is only 200 years old, each of the castle's buildings has a distinctive artistic value. Based on these findings, the official report by UNESCO's World Heritage Committee concluded that Suwon *Hwaseong* is the epitome of military architecture in the Far East, consisting of scientific, rational structures designed for practical use. It is also notable for serving military, political, and commercial functions, as well as utilizing both flat and hilly terrain to optimize natural defenses.

Hwaseong's Cultural and Historical Significance

Besides its distinction as a work of architecture, *Hwaseong* also has a profound historical significance. The king who commissioned it, Choson Dynasty's 22nd monarch Chongjo (1752~1800) was deeply devoted to his father, Sado Seja, who had been installed as Crown Prince only a year after his birth. Devoted to literature during his youth, Sado Seja showed great intellectual promise, and would often share his compositions in poetry and prose with court ministers. However, due to a deep-rooted fear of his father King Yongjo, he would at times exhibit eccentric behavior, bordering on insanity, and thus incurred his father's anger. Tragically, he died at the young age of 28, the victim of a court intrigue. The young Chongjo, only eleven at the time, experienced grief and longing for his father until his old age.

Succeeding his grandfather Yongjo at the age of 25 in 1776, Chongjo regularly paid visits to his father's tomb. In 1789 he had the tomb moved to the mountain district behind the village of Suwon, then known as one of the most auspicious burial grounds in Korea. He asked the villagers to move to the new Suwon district, providing them with money for transport and ready accommodation. New Suwon was the first planned city in the history of Korea. Royal villas, government offices and travel inns came to be built in the area, and as settlers moved in, the new castle town of Suwon was born.

Unfailingly every year, Chongjo would pay his respects before his father's place of burial. The visit in 1795 was a very special one, as it was the year of his mother's 60's birthday[18]. Had his father Sado Seja been alive, he would have held 60th birthday celebrations for both his parents, as they were of the same age. King Chongjo commemorated the important occasion with a grand display at *Hwaseong* Fortress, near the burial grounds of his father. The detailed records of this event (*Uigwe*) are a rich storehouse of historical information concerning traditional royal ceremonies, music and dance.

Until the 17th century, national defense projects were achieved by means of compulsory labor. Ordinary citizens providing manual assistance were expected to bring their own food, while skilled craftsmen received only partial contributions towards their living expenses. Chong Yak-yong, who was in overall charge of the construction of *Hwaseong*, argued that a system of wage labor based on performance should replace the old one. His proposals were adopted in full by King Chongjo, who was a benevolent monarch.

Compulsory labor was inefficient, whereas wage-labor was not only effective,

---

[18] In East Asia, the first and sixtieth birthdays are considered the most important.

King Chongjo held a grand banquet on his mother's 60th birthday at *Hwaseong* Fortress. (A page from *Uigwe*)

but also served as a relief program to support struggling farmers. The construction of Suwon *Hwaseong* was therefore not an onerous burden on the public, but like President Roosevelt's Tennessee regeneration program, became a national project that revived the economy and restored the fortunes of impoverished citizens. For farmers without land, the Fortress' construction was an excellent source of work, and gave life and prosperity to the neighborhood of Suwon.

Over the two years and eight months of the construction, the King supported the workers with great care and encouragement. On eleven occasions, he gave special feasts, and ordered extra supplies and equipment in the extreme weather conditions of summer and winter. During the winter months, he gave every worker a fur hat and a roll of cotton to line his clothes, and for the hottest periods, he had 4,000 packs of medicine specially prepared as a precaution against the effects of the heat.

Besides acting as the capital Seoul's southern defensive base, King Chongjo also wanted to develop Suwon into a large city with a healthy economy. Established on level ground and located ideally for transport, Suwon had the potential to thrive as a financially independent city. In order to attract business, the Choson government adopted a raft of policies, ranging from direct funding to the granting of exclusive international trading rights over certain products. After the passing of several years, 63 households grew to around 1000, and the quiet rural village became a centre of commerce, home to every kind of trade.

When the fortress was completed in October 1796, King Chongjo ordered an account of its construction to be written, and five years later the *Hwaseong Fortress Uigwe*[19] was published. The depth of the records and detail of the illustrations and diagrams is astonishing. In addition to standard items such as project duration, staffing levels, and the tools and machines used, the book goes

---

[19] *Uigwe* were highly detailed procedural records, prepared whenever an important ceremony was held or an important building was constructed.

so far as to list even the number and unit price of the nails, as well as the location, days worked, and daily pay of each individual worker.

This demonstrates the meticulous effort that went into documentation of the project, as well as its actual execution, and the organised way in which the project was approached. The *Uigwe* provides exact explanations of the fortress' facilities, arranged in a logical manner. Together with diagrams for the interior and exterior, it even includes perspective drawings, enabling us today to determine how *Hwaseong* was constructed. This was demonstrated when the *Hwaseong Fortress Uigwe* was used to restore the fortress in 1975. Together with other *Uigwe*, this document was inscribed in the UNESCO Memory of the World Register in 2007.

42. The Science of Palace Architecture

Injong Hall in Changdok Palace was used for important celebrations and ceremonies, and official receptions were held in the forecourt. The forecourt is of particular interest, as it was clearly built to maximize the quality of the acoustics. Both the eaves of the building which overlook the forecourt and the granite paving slabs of the floor make use of the principle of 'diffuse reflection' to ensure even distribution of sound, similar in respects to techniques used in modern theatres. The cloisters which surround the forecourt served to amplify and extend the sound to improve the quality still further. The paving stones also distributed light evenly, making the interior of the forecourt unusually bright. Even the soil beneath the slabs was chosen carefully to ensure efficient drainage of rainwater.

Changdok Palace was one of the five palaces of the Choson royal family, and is famous for its beautiful garden. The most important building in the palace was Injong Hall, which served as an audience chamber, and was used to hold important national events such as coronations and royal celebrations. Foreign envoys and delegations were officially received in the forecourt of the hall. At such events, civil officials stood by their rank stone[20] on the eastern side, and military officials on the western side. Recent studies have shown that the Injong Hall and its forecourt were designed with great care, specifically with such events in mind.

It was very important for the entire audience to be able to hear the

---

[20] Stones inscribed with the hierarchical rankings (1 *pum* to 9 *pum*) were erected in the forecourt.

Injong Hall of Changdok Palace

proceedings, and very difficult to ensure this in the days before amplifying speakers. In his paper '*Acoustics of the Injong Hall's Forecourt*', Professor Chon Chin-yong notes that the eaves of the Hall are ideally designed for diffuse reflection[21], and as a result sound spreads well in the courtyard below. Seen from its side, the Hall's eaves extend some way beyond the wall, and curve upwards slightly at the end. This not only has the effect of reflecting the voice of a person speaking at the front of the Hall back to the speaker, but also 'scatters' it throughout the yard. The roof of the Injong Hall is in many ways similar to the acoustic shell found in modern-day theaters, which helps amplify the sound of stage performers for the benefit of the audience and the performers themselves.

The paving stones in the courtyard also played an important acoustic role.

---

[21] Diffuse reflection is the means whereby light or sound is reflected from an uneven or rough surface and scatters or '*diffuses*' in a number of directions.

Sound reflection **Light reflection**

The forecourt is covered with large, thin stone panels, cut from granite. Because granite is very solid, it reflects sound well, and its rough surface ensures that sound is diffused in all directions.

Professor Chon also examined the cloisters around the Hall, which are lined with columns on the inside. When the sound from the speaker's platform reached the cloisters, some of it was reflected back into the yard by the columns, and the sound that travelled through the gaps was reflected by the outer wall, and returned to the yard as well. The cloisters therefore act as a two-stage reflector, having a lengthening effect on the sound. In addition, the eaves of the cloister roofs are designed like the underside of a balcony in a modern theater, amplifying the reflected sounds and making them converge in the forecourt. In terms of structure, Injong is akin to a huge concert hall.

The designers also approached the issue of lighting with wisdom. The Hall appears brighter than usual, because of the granite stone panels used in the forecourt. Of the different minerals comprising granite, white mica gives it a shiny appearance, while quartz (a major component of glass) gives it transparency. The white component of granite reflects light of every wave length, making the Hall appear even brighter.

As with sound, the natural lighting of the Injong Hall is enhanced by the rough surface of the granite stones. Movies can be seen from any seat in a cinema because the cinema screens are based on the principle of diffuse reflection – if one touches the screen, one can feel that it is uneven. Similarly, in the courtyard, light is reflected at uneven angles and spreads out in all directions, meaning that it is distributed evenly at every point in the Hall.

Another notable feature of the palace architecture is its efficient drainage system. Beneath the thin granite floor panels, there is a layer of decomposed granite soil. As Professor Yi Chae-gun of Sangmyong University explains, 'Decomposed granite soil is white clay without any viscosity, and because it consists of large particles, it absorbs and releases water well. It is therefore used in the drainage facilities of modern buildings.'

In the Injong courtyard, the granite soil draws away the rainwater, and to prevent the soil itself being washed away or causing dust, granite panels were laid over the top, leaving an adequate distance in between for drainage. When it rained, the water would travel down from the Hall's roof, pass underground via the granite soil, gather at the catch-pit and pass along the subterranean stone waterways, out of the Palace grounds. In every corner of this traditional work of Korean architecture, hidden wonders can be found.

43. A Treasury of Eastern Medicine

The *Tongui Pogam* was composed by Heo Jun, a court physician, and published in 1613. Known as one of the greatest books in the history of Eastern medicine, it was published and used in many countries including China and Japan, and remains a key reference work for the study of Eastern medicine. Its categorization and ordering of symptoms and remedies under the different human organs affected, rather than the disease itself, was a revolutionary development. It contains insights that in some cases did not enter the medical knowledge of Europe until the twentieth century.

"This book was written by Heo Jun of Choson. Although he is a foreigner from a distant land, distance is no hindrance in the pursuit of learning. The book has been presented to the Emperor for his attention, and it has been acknowledged as the most excellent of medical works. Regrettably, it has until now been confined to the Palace, and ordinary people have found it difficult to become acquainted with its text. A treasure under the Heavens should be for all under the Heavens to enjoy."

- Ling Yu, a Chinese scholar, from his foreword to the Chinese edition of the *Tongui Pogam*

First published in Korea in 1613, *Tongui Pogam* (Precious Mirror of Eastern Medicine) has been acclaimed as one of the greatest books in the history of medical literature, and widely read throughout East Asia. To date, it has been reprinted more than 30 times in China – a new edition nearly every decade – and it was placed in wide circulation by the shoguns in Japan. *Tongui Pogam* remains a steady seller today, and is one of the main reference textbooks for students of Eastern medicine.

It is not unusual to study books written hundreds of years ago. The works of Shakespeare, for example, are still enjoyed not only in their written form, but also on the stage and in cinemas. Unlike literature and philosophy, however, which explore universal human issues that do not change, medicine is a branch of science in which new knowledge rapidly replaces the old. The fact that a medical text from 400 years ago still has authority in this modern age is therefore truly remarkable.

A New Era in Eastern Medical Literature

Tongui Pogam was written by the royal physician Heo Jun (1545~1615) at the commission of King Sonjo. The book, which took Heo Jun 14 years to complete, reviews the entire history of medicine in East Asia, from the time of the Yellow Emperor, believed to have founded the principles of medicine, to the 17th century AD, and covers 2,000 symptoms, 1,400 medicines, 4,000 prescriptions, hundreds of acupuncture techniques, and also advice for good health. There are many publications that surpass the *Tongui Pogam* in terms of length. Its accuracy and practicability, however, achieved by comparing many complex medical treatises and extracting the most efficient and reliable information based on the author's own medical experiences, make the book a true masterpiece.

Comprising 25 volumes in total, *Tongui Pogam* is arranged under five headings: *Internal Organs, External Organs, Other Diseases, Prescription of Medicine,* and *Acupuncture and Moxibustion.* The main diseases are discussed in the first two sections. More obscure conditions, or those specific to infants or females, are dealt with in the third, while the final two sections introduce substances with medicinal properties as well as acupuncture techniques for the cure of diseases.

Briedie Andrews and Elisabeth Lee Hsu, researchers at the Needham Research Institute of Cambridge University, have observed that the structure of the *Tongui Pogam* is different from that of other medical texts of East Asia. In the book, Heo Jun categorized diseases under the human organs primarily affected. Such ordering might seem very natural, but it was in fact an entirely new approach, never previously used in China or Korea. This change in perspective could be compared to the story of the 'Egg of Columbus' – simple and obvious only after it has been explained.

Previous medical texts focused mainly on the treatment of different diseases, and did not attempt a comprehensive understanding of the body itself. When the 'body' is the starting point and not the 'disease', the study of medicine is given far more coherence and order. In this way, the *Tongui Pogam* was able to make clearer distinctions between the two, and consequently proved to be more useful in the study and application of methods for maintaining health, as well the treatments of various ailments.

By compiling *Tongui Pogam*, Heo Jun made a great contribution to the systematic organization of Eastern medicine. In the first Chinese edition of the *Tongui Pogam* (1747), the editor wrote, 'Ever since I learned to read, I have studied medical literature with zeal, but regrettably I was never able to gain a holistic understanding of medicine. I came across *Tongui Pogam*, written by Heo Jun, and found that its analysis of the properties of drugs is exceptionally well-ordered, in that the prescription is dialectically deduced from a detailed description of the patient's symptoms and changing condition. In a mountain of medical literature, it was a hidden treasure trove.' In the *Chinese Pharmaceutical Encyclopaedia*, published in 1935, *Tongui Pogam* is described as follows, 'Its coverage is vast, its sequence logical, and it is a monumental piece of work in the field of medicine.'

Until the 18th century, Japanese envoys sought after medical texts above all else during their stay in Korea. The *Tongui Pogam* was widely read by Japanese medical practitioners after it was introduced to the country in 1651, and a Japanese version was published in 1724, under the title *Revised Tongui Pogam*. There were several other editions afterwards, and the 1799 edition from Osaka contains the following postscript by Minamotono Motodouru, a medical researcher. '[The *Tongui Pogam*] places every theory, from the past to the present, at one's fingertips, and will be of great help as a reference guide to anyone engaged in a medical career…It is a divine book, which will keep people from harm, and contains the secrets of the medical profession.'

In 1748, a Korean diplomatic delegation had just arrived at Namba in Japan when one of its members fell ill and sought attention from a local doctor. When the traveling party expressed some misgiving about entrusting him to a foreign physician, whose methods were unfamiliar to them, the Japanese doctor indignantly asked how his medical practice could be doubted when it was based on Heo Jun's *Tongui Pogam*. The sick envoy is said to have made a good recovery under his care, and the Japanese doctor received the warm thanks of everyone.

Tongui Pogam Lives On

In the history of medicine, the 16th and 17th centuries were a time of great progress. In Western Europe, the Belgian anatomist Andreas Vesalius (1514~1564) laid the foundations of modern medicine with his *De Humanis Corporis Fabrica*. Published in Basel in 1543, it contained 600 pages of text and more than 300 appended human anatomical diagrams. Originally written in Latin, *Fabrica* was translated into many languages and was a standard textbook not only in the field of anatomy but across the whole of medicine. Based on a dissection of the human body, the book fundamentally changed the way the body was viewed.

These achievements were built upon by William Harvey (1578~1657), an English physician credited as the first Western doctor to describe the circulation of blood, and regarded as the father of modern physiology. Like Heo Jun, he was the physician to the king and left behind a celebrated medical work, the *Exercitatio Anatomica de Motu Cordis et Sanguinis in Animalibus* (1628). Through a combination of observation, inference, and an experiment showing the swelling of veins in a ligated arm, he proved the theory of systemic circulation, resolving the age-long question of 'where blood flows to'.

At the time that Heo Jun was alive in Korea therefore, detailed analysis and clearer appreciation of bodily structures, as well as experimental corroboration of physiological mechanisms, were taking place in 17th century Europe. The understanding of pathology remained basic, however, and both pharmacology and therapeutics were relatively underdeveloped, with Galen's theory of the four humors (the bodily fluids blood, phlegm, choler and melancholy) still dominant in this branch of medicine. Few drugs were available, and treatments tended to be fairly basic, such as the inducement of bowel movements with laxatives.

By comparison, the understanding of pathological conditions evident in *Tongui Pogam* is vast and profound, as are the methods of treatment, ranging from drugs to acupuncture and moxibustion. It was only established in the 20th century that hepatitis spreads by contact with infected blood, and yet this is noted by Heo Jun in the *Tongui Pogam*. Moreover, while therapeutics in the West began to develop rapidly at the close of 19th century, the methods of treatment prescribed by *Tongui Pogam* in the 17th century are still being used today.

By far the greatest merit of *Tongui Pogam* is that it has saved countless lives. Furthermore, its benefits have not been restricted to the wealthy and the privileged, but were available to ordinary people as well. Because medicinal ingredients were costly, the poor often suffered grave illnesses without any medication. Heo Jun sought ways to enhance the effectiveness of inexpensive medicinal ingredients that could be obtained easily. As well as prescribing treatments that combined numerous medicines, he also included many prescriptions which involved only one ingredient.

Although Heo Jun is famous for leaving behind a detailed work on oriental medicine, his great goal was to find a medicine that everyone could use. He wrote other books as well, many of which concern contagious diseases. Remembering this noble spirit, Koreans hold the memory of Heo Jun in admiration and respect to this day.

44. *Bulgogi*

Despite its name, which means 'fire-meat', *Bulgogi* is popular for its soft texture and mild yet distinctive taste. The secret lies in the careful preparation process of cutting, tenderizing, and marinating the meat. It is a healthy dish as well as a tasty one: the marinade of soy sauce and sugar suppresses the formation of unhealthy cholesterol oxidization products (COPs), and its other ingredients are healthy as well, containing a range of key vitamins and beneficial organic compounds which aid digestion. Although a meat dish, it is generally eaten in a vegetable wrap, making it a nutritionally balanced meal.

Bulgogi is the most famous and beloved of Korean beef dishes. Its texture is tender and sweet, and people generally become devoted to it after tasting it just once.

The literal translation of *Bulgogi* is 'fire-meat' (*bul-gogi*). Its origins can be traced back to the Koguryo period (BC 37 – AD 668). The people of Koguryo used to have a beef dish called *maekjok*, which was prepared by marinating skewered beef in soy sauce and garlic and grilling it over a fire. The recipe travelled to China, and gained a reputation as something of a delicacy. During the Six Dynasties Period, Gan Bao recorded in his book, *In Search of the Supernatural*: '*Maekjok* is a foreign dish, but the Chinese enjoy it greatly, and always serve it at parties hosted by the wealthy or high-ranking.'

When Buddhism was adopted as the state religion during the 4th century, meat dishes became less common in Korea, as Buddhism strictly prohibits the taking of life. During the 13th century, the practice of eating meat was revived following the Mongol invasions. For the nomadic Mongols, meat was a staple food, and the culture of Korea was naturally influenced by their customs. In the capital city of Kaesong, a centre of international trade and commerce, various meat dishes gained popularity. In time, this revival led to the appearance of a beef dish reserved for the royal palace called *nobiani*, which later became known as *Bulgogi*.

The unique taste of *Bulgogi* has appealed to people from many different countries. The secret of its taste lies in the cooking process and the preparation of the meat. Traditionally, the tender and less fatty portion of sirloin or short ribs have been used for *Bulgogi*. The fat and the tendons are carefully removed from the meat. To tenderize the beef, one gently pats the lean meat with the back of a knife. During this process of cutting and tenderizing, the meat becomes much softer and the marinating is more effective as a result. The marinade consists of pear juice and rice wine (red wine can also be used). During the marinating process, the meat is softened by enzymes, making it easier to digest. The meat is then combined with a mixture of soy sauce, chopped spring onion, minced garlic and ginger, powdered sesame, salt, pepper, and sesame oil. After twelve hours the meat is ready to be grilled or sautéed in a pan without oil. Since *Bulgogi* is marinated before it is grilled, no other sauce needs to be prepared. The grilled meat has a mild yet distinctive taste.

Research has shown that marinating meat in sugar and soy sauce before grilling is better for one's health. In June 2006, the Journal of Agriculture and Food Chemistry, published by the American Chemical Society, released findings showing that cooking meat with sugar and soy sauce suppresses the formation of cholesterol oxidation products (COP). These are generally formed when food containing a high level of cholesterol is heated or cooked. It is known that an excessive quantity of COPs can damage cells in the body and cause heart disease or cancer.

In order to research the effects of marinated meat and the formation of COPs, a team of researchers at Taiwan's Fujian University prepared a sample of pork and hard boiled egg in three different marinades, the first using soy sauce, the second using sugar, and the third using a combination of both.

According to their research, when meat is marinated in soy sauce or sugar, the formation of COPs decreases. The role of the sugar was found to be particularly important.

Professor Chen, who led the research team, explained that the sugar and soy sauce marinade produce a browning reaction product which acts as an anti-oxidant, neutralizing COPs. In addition, beneficial nutrients contained in soy sauce, such as isoflavones, also suppress the formation of COPs. This proves that marinated meat dishes are not only tasty, but good for one's health as well.

It should also be noted that while the marinade used for *Bulgogi* contains soy sauce and sugar, the spring onion, garlic, ginger, and sesame oil are also very healthy ingredients. Not only do they counteract the odor of the meat, as well as tenderizing it and giving it a pleasant flavor, but they also enhance its health benefits.

Sesame oil contains many beneficial unsaturated fatty acids such as linolenic acid, which helps suppress cholesterol. Sesame itself contains acids which suppress cholesterol and assist bowel movement. It also contains high levels of calcium, iron, and Vitamin B1 and B2. Garlic helps reduce cholesterol and total fat in the liver and blood serum. The allicin contained in it has an antibacterial effect, helping the production of digestive enzymes in the gastric juices. It also assists the intestinal movements and overall digestion. *Bulgogi* is therefore suitable even for those with weak digestive systems, such as the old or very young.

The ssam is the finishing touch in the preparation of *Bulgogi*. Ssam is a kind of vegetable wrap, made with vegetable leaves such as lettuce, sesame, or crown daisy, and is generally eaten with ssamjang sauce. The ssamjang consists of soybean paste (made with fermented soybeans) and hot pepper. It is therefore an excellent fermented food, and contributes both to the taste and the nutritional value of the ssam. As the meat is eaten in a vegetable wrap, moreover, the meal is nutritionally balanced, and so counteracts the onset of arterial diseases, hypertension, and cancer. If its taste, nutritional value, and health benefits are considered together, there is no better meat dish than *Bulgogi*.

***Bulgogi* with Ssam**

How To Make *Bulgogi*

Ingredients

1 lb beef (sirloin or short ribs), thinly sliced

Marinade sauce:

A. 4 tbs Korean pear juice & 1 tbs red wine

B. 4 tbs dark soy sauce & 1 1/2 tbs honey or sugar

C. 2 tbs chopped scallions, 2 tbs minced garlic, 1 tbs sesame oil, pinch of
black pepper, 5 or 6 mid-size mushrooms (Button mushroom) and 1/2 an
onion (add when pan-frying)

Recipe

1. Cut the beef into bite-size pieces. Place the meat in a strainer and sprinkle water to remove the blood.

2. To tenderize the beef, gently pat the meat with the back of a knife.

3. Mix the pear juice and red wine in a bowl. Add beef to the mixture of wine and pear juice, and meanwhile prepare the marinade sauce.

4. Mix the dark soy sauce and honey in a bowl and stir until the honey completely dissolves. Add scallions, garlic, sesame oil and black pepper to the dark soy sauce and honey mixture.

5. Add the soy sauce and honey marinade to the meat, wine and pear juice, and allow to marinate for 12 hours.

6. Grill or pan-fry the marinated beef without oil.

7. Serve *Bulgogi* with ssam, vegetables and ssamjang sauce.

45. *Kimchi*

Kimchi, a Korean method of preserving vegetables by fermentation, is recognized as one of the five healthiest foods in the world. Eaten for over 2000 years in the Korean peninsula, it is prepared in many different ways, and is found at every Korean meal. It is credited with keeping obesity at bay in Korea, and furthermore has been shown to combat stress and to slow the ageing process, as well as fighting cancer and a wide variety of deadly conditions such as SARS and bird flu. This is due to the many healthy ingredients it contains, and its high concentration of beneficial lactobacilli.

In March 2006, Health Magazine of the USA selected the five healthiest foods in the world. The results were: Spanish olive oil, Japanese soy, Greek yogurt, Indian lentils, and Korean *Kimchi*. In the article, *Kimchi* was described as follows, 'Loaded with key vitamins, *Kimchi* contains healthy bacteria that aid digestion. It's part of a high-fiber, low-fat diet that has kept obesity at bay in Korea.'

According to the most recent OECD health data, Korea has the lowest rate of obesity among all the OECD countries, with only 3.5% of the adult population categorized as obese. The country with the highest level was the United States, with obesity affecting 34% of the population, followed by Mexico (30%) and the UK (24%).

Kimchi is a traditional fermented vegetable dish. It is an important part of the Korean diet and part of every Korean meal. According to historical records, *Kimchi* has been eaten for at least 2,000 years in the Korean peninsula. There are over 200 varieties, and many dishes are based on *Kimchi*, such as *Kimchi* stew,

Baechu *Kimchi* (Korean cabbage *Kimchi*) is the most common type of *Kimchi*. It is usually eaten as a side dish.

Kimchi pancakes, *Kimchi* stir-fried rice, *Kimchi* mandu (dumplings), *Kimchi* rolls, and *Kimchi* burgers. The average Korean consumes about 30 kilograms (67 pounds) of *Kimchi* per year. It is no exaggeration to say that *Kimchi* is a cultural symbol as well as one of the foundations of Korean cuisine.

The traditional Korean diet is mainly vegetarian. As Korea is a country with four distinct seasons, various ways of preserving vegetables were developed in order to ensure that they were available during the cold winter days when they could not easily be grown. The most famous of these preservation methods is the one used to make *Kimchi*.

As the winter approached, people would join their relatives and neighbors in making large quantities of *Kimchi* using Korean cabbages. In the old days, *Kimchi* was kept in earthenware jars and stored underground. Small portions would be taken from the jar throughout the winter. This was the ideal way to preserve *Kimchi* over long periods of time, as it was not exposed to the air, and the temperature was constant, never falling below freezing point. Storing the *Kimchi* in natural earthen jars improved its taste and enhanced its nutritional value by assisting the fermentation process.

These days most households use special refrigerators designed for storing *Kimchi*. Whilst ordinary refrigerators have doors at the front, the doors of the *Kimchi* refrigerators open at the top, like the covers of the earthen jars. This positioning is intended to help minimize the outflow of cold air, and keep the temperature inside the refrigerator stable. Ordinary refrigerators operate by circulating cold air, which means that fruits and vegetables can become dry. A *Kimchi* refrigerator employs a direct cooling method, using the actual surfaces of the storage area, thereby preserving the freshness of *Kimchi* for a much longer period of time.

Kimchi is made by pickling vegetables such as radish, cabbage, and cucumber in salt, and mixing them with other flavored ingredients such as chili pepper powder, garlic, scallion, ginger, and pickled seafood. Adding these various ingredients is key to making the *Kimchi* tasty and nutritious, and once they have been added, the jar can be sealed and fermented over a period of time.

Although in many other cultures vegetables are pickled, such as Chinese paocai and Japanese zukemono in the East, or cucumber pickles and sauerkraut in the West, in which vinegar and salt are mainly used, *Kimchi* produces greater quantities of beneficial lactobacilli and valuable bioactive substances than any of them.

In 1999, Fuji Television broadcast a documentary which showed that Korean *Kimchi* contained 167 times more lactobacilli than its Japanese counterpart 'kimuchi'. As a result, there was a sudden increase in the popularity of *Kimchi* in Japan. One gram of well-fermented *Kimchi* contains about one hundred million lactobacilli, far greater than the amount contained in yoghurt. These lactobacilli help to cleanse the large intestine by assisting the growth of beneficial micro-organisms and suppressing harmful bacteria.

Furthermore, since *Kimchi* is rich in anti-oxidants such as Vitamin C, beta carotene, phenol compounds, and chlorophyll, it is very effective in reducing stress. In a study carried out by Professor Lee Jongmi of Ewha Women's

University, when a mouse under stress was fed with a preparation containing 5% *Kimchi*, its blood corticosterone (a hormone that indicates the stress level) was reduced by 30.4%.

Kimchi is also known to slow the process of ageing in the skin. Professor Park Kunyoung of Pusan University tested the skin cell thickness of mice fed with *Kimchi* for sixteen weeks. Skin usually becomes drier and thinner with age, but the skin cells of the mice that were fed with *Kimchi* showed an increase in thickness of more than 24% compared to the mice that were given ordinary food. Also, it appeared that the formation of new collagen (fibrous structural protein that forms skin, bone and so on) in the derma structure increased, indicating anti-ageing effects on the skin as well, from *Kimchi*

One of the reasons that *Kimchi* has recently gained an international reputation is its role in the SARS (Severe Acute Respiratory Syndrome) outbreak of 2003, the first epidemic of the 21st century. After its initial occurrence in November 2002, it spread to 29 countries in just a few months. Before the World Health Organization (WHO) officially declared the world 'SARS free' in July 2003, the virus had claimed many lives and caused worldwide anxiety.

95% of SARS cases were concentrated in Asia, particularly in China and the surrounding countries. Surprisingly, not a single case of SARS was reported in Korea, even though the country borders with China. From this point on, researchers began to pay more attention to *Kimchi*, the daily food of Koreans, firstly for its potential as a defense against SARS, and secondly for its general positive effects on the immune system.

Two years after the outbreak, in March 2005, major media companies, such as BBC and ABC, reported that scientists had identified the possibility that *Kimchi* may help in the fight against Avian Influenza (Bird Flu). A research team lead by Professor Kang Sawook of Seoul National University fed the lactobacillus culture fluid extracted from *Kimchi* to chickens that were infected with the virus. According to their research, the chickens that were fed only with regular food had a survival rate of 54%, whereas those that were fed with the extract of *Kimchi* had a survival rate of 85%. In the case of the chickens fed normally, the virus reduced their egg-laying capacity to 50%, but when fed with the *Kimchi* extract, this increased again to 85%.

In November 2006, Dr. Lee Jong-kyung of the Korea Food Research Institute found that when salmonella, O-157, and vibrio bacteria were introduced into a sample of well-fermented *Kimchi* (pH 4.4), 99% of the bacteria were destroyed within 4 hours, and the vibrio bacteria within 10 minutes. It also became clear that when *Kimchi* is consumed with meat or fish, it can help prevent food poisoning.

Kimchi's anti-cancer properties are also the focus of growing interest. Professor Park of Pusan University injected *Kimchi*'s MSF extract into mice with cancer cell transplants. After one month, the mice that were fed normally had an average tumor weight of 4.3 grams, whereas the group that were fed with *Kimchi* extract had an average tumor weight of 2.0 grams, showing that *Kimchi* may help suppress the growth of a tumor.

The methanol extract of *Kimchi* showed anti-mutative effect on carcinogenic substances not only in animal testing, but also in in vitro testing as well. In many other experiments, *Kimchi* extract has been shown to suppress the growth of cancer cells or weaken the virulent effect of carcinogens.

The amazing benefits of *Kimchi* are due to the combined medicinal value of its individual ingredients. Although the most well-known variety of *Kimchi* is made with cabbage, variants of the dish include radish, garlic stalks, eggplant, and mustard leaf, and other ingredients. Minced ginger, garlic, chili pepper powder, and pickled seafood are added to the main ingredients for flavoring, and are beneficial for the body in and of themselves.

Professor Chang Ja-jun of Seoul National University's College of Medicine discovered that each of *Kimchi*'s ingredients, such as cabbage, chili pepper, and garlic, were highly effective in preventing various types of cancer. Capsaicin, for

Various Types of _Kimchi_

example, which is responsible for chili peppers' spicy taste, is known to suppress lung cancer. Allicin, contained in garlic, is known to suppress liver cancer, stomach cancer, bladder cancer, and thyroid cancer. Indole-3-carbinol, contained in cabbage, is also known to suppress stomach cancer.

Studies in other countries have produced similar results. In 1999, Harvard Medical School reported that eating cabbage and broccoli can reduce the risk of bladder cancer. The U.S. National Cancer Institute chose garlic as the number one anti-cancer ingredient out of a selection of 40 different foods. As the health benefits of *Kimchi* are recognized by researchers, it has gained a worldwide reputation as one of the most effective health foods, and a leading example of 'natural' medicine.

Kimchi reaches its optimum taste and nutritional value when it has been fermented for two to three weeks at a low temperature, between 2 - 7°C. Unfermented *Kimchi* has about 10,000 lactobacilli per milliliter. After it is fermented, the number of lactobacilli increases to between 63 and 100 million per milliter – up to one thousand times. The amount of Vitamin B1 and B2 in the vegetable ingredients decreases slightly when they are first made into *Kimchi*, but after about three weeks it increases to twice the original amount. The amount of Vitamin C also decreases slightly when fermentation begins, but then reaches its peak after the second week of fermentation.

Kimchi also has beneficial effects in terms of weight loss. According to Professor Park, this effect is largely due to the capsaicin in the chili pepper. However, when other ingredients are added, such as garlic, ginger, and radish, and fermentation takes place, the effects are increased.

In an experiment with groups of white mice put on a high-fat diet for four weeks, the group fed with chili pepper and the group fed with *Kimchi* lost a significant amount of weight compared to the group fed on the high-fat diet alone. Notably, the mice fed with the *Kimchi* and high-fat diet maintained a similar weight to the group on regular feed. (Table 1)

Table 1. Variation in Weight after Four Weeks

Weight (g)	Regular Food	High-Fat Food	High-Fat Food with 5% Chili Pepper Powder	High-Fat Food with 10% Kimchi*
Initial Weight	171.4	170.3	170.7	171.4
Final weight	305.7	338.7	311	302.5

* The 10% *Kimchi* diet contained the same level of red chili pepper powder as the 5% chili powder diet alone.

As shown here, *Kimchi* is filled with natural vitality. It is one of the foods that may provide an answer to the various adult conditions, such as obesity, that have resulted from modern society's eating habits. *Kimchi* can be purchased from Asian grocery stores, and even at some of the larger supermarkets. If you are uncertain how to eat *Kimchi*, Health Magazine recommends adding it to scrambled egg, tomato, and mushrooms. *Kimchi* can also be eaten as a baked potato filling. Eating a few pieces of *Kimchi* with a meal of steak or other high-fat food will help to cleanse the palate and assist digestion.

46. Fermented Soy Food

Fermentation is a natural method of preserving food, and is known to contribute to long life. Traditional fermented dishes such as *doenjang* and *Kimchi* form the basis of the Korean diet. In the case of soybean-based dishes such as *doenjang*, the health benefits of soybeans are increased by the process of fermentation, and can help prevent heart disease, obesity, and a wide range of cancers.

Certain cities and regions around the world are known for the longevity of their inhabitants. In many of these places, such as Smolyan in Bulgaria, Hunza in Pakistan, or the countries of the Caucasus, people consume fermented milk products as part of their daily diet. Among the five healthiest foods in the world chosen by *Health* magazine in a recent survey, three are prepared by means of fermentation. Why are fermented foods so good for the body?

The majority of mass-produced food items today have long expiry dates, thanks to artificial processes such as pasteurization, freezing, or adding preservatives. Adding preservatives is undoubtedly bad for the body. While pasteurization removes harmful bacteria, it also eradicates beneficial bacteria, resulting in food that is lifeless. Freezing also has the effect of removing freshness from food.

Fermentation, on the other hand, extends the life of food using natural micro-organisms instead of artificial processes, and does not have harmful effects on health. In general, when food is fermented, its nutritional value increases, and the texture and flavor is enhanced. More importantly, the beneficial bacteria produced during the fermentation process eradicate harmful substances and infections, boost the body's immune and digestive systems, and help prevent diseases such as cancer. Accordingly, many nutritionists today are performing research on traditional fermented foods in order to find solutions to current disorders such as obesity and other adult diseases.

The Origins of Soybean Fermentation

70% of Korean food is naturally fermented. Over 200 types of *Kimchi*, numerous other pickled vegetables, the popular rice drink *shikhye*, various types of salted seafood preserves, and the three major sauces (soy sauce, soybean paste, chili pepper paste) are all prepared by means of fermentation. It is fair to say that fermented food products are the foundation of a Korean diet.

According to the Chinese historical work *Records of Three Kingdoms*, written in the 3rd century, the people of Koguryo, one of the three ancient kingdoms of Korea, were skilled in preparing fermented dishes. The Korean *History of the Three Kingdoms* states that at the wedding of the Silla King Sinmun, the gifts brought by the bride to her new in-laws included liquor, fermented soybean paste, and fermented vegetables and seafood.

Doenjang Stew

In a survey conducted in Korea in May 2004, the five most popular foods by vote were *doenjang* stew (22.7%), *kimchi* stew (17.5%), *kimchi* (16.2%), *bulgogi* (8.2%), and *bibimbap* (5.4%). The top three foods by popularity – *kimchi* stew, *kimchi*, and *doenjang* – making up more than half (56.4%) of the vote, are made by fermentation.

Fermented soybean blocks *meju* and soybean paste *doenjang*

Doenjang stew, the favorite, is prepared with fermented soybean paste, which is rich in nutrition, and also mushrooms, tofu, and various vegetables. It is not only good to taste, but it is also known as a health food that can prevent diseases and even slow the ageing process. The following tale about how *doenjang* was created has been preserved as part of the Buddhist tradition of Korea:

During the period of Old Choson (2333 BC~108 BC) in Korea, there lived an enlightened master. He always pondered as to how human beings might commit less sin. The master concluded that people committed sins because their minds were not at ease. With this realization, he wondered if there was any food that could calm people's minds and help them feel gratitude to the heavens, so that they would commit fewer sins simply by eating it. Through his devoted prayers and meditation, he realized that he should use soybeans to create this special food, since soybeans were very nutritious and easy to grow. He first soaked the soybeans for about a day, and then boiled them at a low heat for roughly twelve hours. He then ground the soybeans and shaped them into blocks. These bean blocks were hung under the eaves of a house and dried by sunlight and wind. By allowing them to receive the sunlight, the master let the bean blocks absorb the energy of the heavens. By letting them dry in the wind, he exposed them to the breath of the Buddha. When the fermentation was complete, they were soaked in saline water. Through the salt, the energy of the sea was added, and by the water, the bean blocks were suspended in the clear mind of the Buddha. *Doenjang* was created with the enlightened master's compassionate and selfless wish to help people commit fewer sins, and is filled with the grace of nature, the heavens, and Buddha.

The soybean has its origins in North East Asia, specifically southern Manchuria and the northern Korean peninsula, where an ancient Korean state was established a thousand years ago. Archeologists and historians have concluded that soybeans were first farmed around 2,000 B.C., and fermented soy food was developed around 1,500 B.C. before spreading to other East Asian countries. An ancient Chinese classic book *Shi Jin* records that soybeans were introduced into China from Manchuria around the 7th century B.C. In Japanese history, the first mention of fermented soybean paste occurs in the *Shosoin Documents*, published around the mid 8th century A.D. The well-known Japanese soybean paste 'miso' comes from the Korean word 'misun' and 'miljo.'

A *meju* is a block of fermented soybean, and the main ingredient for soy sauce, soybean paste, and chili paste. *Meju* are made with a fresh crop of soybeans in early winter. After soaking the soybeans in water for about a day, they are fully boiled in water, crushed in a mortar, and shaped into blocks. When these soybean blocks are bound with rice straw and hung beneath the eaves of a house, the process of fermentation begins, with the growth of beneficial fungi, and the process continues over the winter. The *meju* are then put into an earthen jar and soaked in saline water. They are placed in an area with plenty of sunshine and fermented again for 30 to 40 days.

The liquid that is produced in the fermentation process becomes soy sauce, and what remains is made into *doenjang*, or fermented bean paste. Whereas in China and Japan wheat or rice is added, Korean *doenjang* is made only with soybeans. While soy sauce and soybean paste are common in East Asia, *kochujang*, or chili pepper paste, is unique to Korea. It has a sweet and spicy taste, and is made by adding chili powder and *meju* powder to other grains such as sweet rice, barley, wheat, and millet.

The Benefits of Fermented Soy Food

In 1925, on a visit to the United States, Sir John McNee, a British doctor, remarked in a letter to a friend that he had been surprised to see two patients with coronary heart disease during his stay. In other words, less than one hundred years ago coronary heart disease was regarded as a 'rare' condition. Nowadays, it has become one of the most common forms of cardiovascular disease, the leading cause of death in America and most European countries.[22]

In October 1999, the US Food and Drug Administration (FDA) authorized the labeling of foods containing soy protein as conducive to reducing the risk of coronary heart disease. The protein content of soybean is about 40%, the highest level found among crops. It is also rich in eight essential amino acids that the body cannot produce for itself. High quality soy protein is almost equivalent to the protein found in meat and dairy products, but unlike animal protein it is low in saturated fat and free from cholesterol.

Besides this, the rich saponin and Vitamin E content in soybeans is known to

---

[22] Messina, M. J. 'Soyfoods: Their Roles in Disease Prevention and Treatment,' *Soybeans, Chemistry, Technology, and Utilization*, New York: Chapman and Hall, 1997.

prevent liver spots and assist blood circulation. Vitamin E, in particular, decreases levels of bad cholesterol and neutral fat. According to some researchers, soy protein and soy isoflavones promote bone health and prevent or minimize menopause symptoms such as hot flashes. Most notably, soy foods are increasingly recognized as having a potential role in the prevention and treatment of a wide range of cancers.

The health benefits of soybeans are dramatically increased by fermentation. Uncooked beans have an absorption rate of 55% when digested, versus 65% for boiled beans. However, when beans are fermented with natural enzymes secreted from micro-organisms, proteins that are difficult to digest are dissolved into a low molecular compound, and the absorption rate increases to 85%. Nutritional inhibitors such as *trypsin* are also completely removed during the fermentation process, resulting in improved digestibility and more effective nutritional usage within the body.

Even after soybeans products such as soy sauce, soybean paste, and chili paste have been prepared, the fermentation process continues, enhancing the taste, nutrition, and health benefits of the final dish. According to the Korean Food Research Institute's analysis, one year old soy sauce contains 43mg of amino nitrogen in every 100 grams. In two year old soy sauce, 680mg of amino nitrogen was found – a 16-fold increase. Amino nitrogen is an intermediary by-product produced when protein breaks down into amino acid. The more amino nitrogen there is, the better the taste. It also increases the nutritional value and absorption rate of fermented soybean foods. This scientific research is proof of the Korean adage, "Friendship and the taste of *jang* [fermented soy products] improve with age."

Researchers have discovered the anti-cancer effects of soybeans also increase when they are fermented. In 1999, Professor Kun-young Park of Pusan University performed an experiment with mice injected with sarcoma 180 cells. Each mouse was fed on a separate diet for twenty days. The result showed that raw soybeans prolonged the lifespan of a mouse by 11%, *miso* (Japanese soybean paste) by 41%, and *doenjang* by 68%. In other words, the anti-cancer benefits of soybeans increase with fermentation. *Doenjang*, produced with 100% soybeans, was much more effective against cancer than *miso*, which includes rice and wheat.

Fermented soy food has also been shown to have an invaluable role in the fight against obesity. As part of Professor Park's research, a mouse weighing 143 grams was fed with high-fat food for 30 days, and its weight increased to 288 grams. When another mouse was fed a diet consisting of 90% high-fat food and 10% *doenjang*, its weight increased to only 247 grams – 41 grams lighter than the first mouse. The cholesterol content of its liver was also much lower than the mouse that was fed only with high-fat food. Fermented soybeans not only counteract obesity but also help to lower the fat in the intestines. All this indicates that soy food cultured and aged in the fermentation process may well have a significant beneficial impact on a country's health.

47. *Bangjja* Bronzeware

Bangjja bronzeware is ancient form of Korean tableware. It is beautiful to look at, and very durable. The secret of its strength lies in using a unique ratio of copper and tin, which defies modern engineering standards. Thanks to the minerals it naturally produces when water is stored in it, *Bangjja* has beneficial health effects, enhancing the taste of food and counteracting infections such as the lethal O-157 colon bacillus.

As well as fermented foods, *Bangjja* bronzeware is another item rich in wisdom and tradition commonly found on the Korean dining table. Each country and region has different foods, and serves them in different dishware. Within East Asia, China traditionally favored porcelain, Japan preferred wooden tableware, and Koreans preferred metal. The hand-forged *Bangjja* bronzeware of Korea has been in use for thousands of years, and is part of its culinary tradition.

In the Shosoin, a Japanese royal treasure house, there are 436 *Bangjja* bowls from 8th century Korea. The ancient Japanese were clearly impressed by their compactness and consistency of design. Up to ten bowls can be stacked together at a time, meaning that their utility is proportionally greater relative to the space required to store them.

Just as the taste of *Kimchi* is unique to Korea, *Bangjja* bronze is found nowhere but in Korea. It is made from an alloy of 78% copper and 22% tin, a ratio that no other nation is known to have used for tableware items.

A ratio of 22% tin is in fact contrary to the conventions of modern science. Tin is a malleable metal which increases the brittleness of an alloy. Its content level is hence limited to 10% in the manufacture of modern materials. *Bangjja*, however, does not break even though it consists of 22% tin. High resistance to corrosion and deterioration meant that it was widely used in Buddhist and

Confucian ceremonies, and even for musical instruments such as gongs and bells.

The secret of *Bangjja's* durability lies in the method used to create it. The tin and copper are mixed together at a high temperature of (1200°C), and the molten mixture is then poured out and hammered into a thin sheet. Once it cools, it is again heated and then hammered. When the molten alloy solidifies, it is initially more than 1 cm thick, and it is converted into a thin sheet by heating and hammering. If it were simply to be hammered and beaten continuously, the sheet would break. However, because the *Bangjja* is produced by heating and hammering *alternately*, the α formations (soft structure) are transformed into β formations (hard structure) through the distribution of tin, as can be seen below from a structural image taken with an SEM (Scanning Electron Microscope). As the process is repeated, more of the β arrangements appear, and as the tin and copper particles become further integrated, potential faultlines disappear, so the material becomes more resistant to shattering.

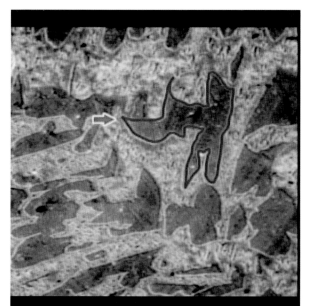

Segregation is almost eliminated.
<After Processing>

Before and after processing

***Bangjja* Tableware**

Another characteristic of *Bangjja* is its beautiful appearance. The whitish gold luster of *Bangjja* gives the illusion that it is actually made of gold. It blends in naturally with the diverse colors of a Korean meal, and brings a feeling of grace and homeliness to the table. If the level of tin is reduced to below 10%, in line with modern guidelines, this color cannot be achieved, and so it remains unique to Korean *Bangjja* produced in accordance with the traditional methods.

Metallic dishware has not been used only in Korea. Ancient Romans also used metal dishes, generally containing lead. The toxic properties of lead seem to have been poorly understood by the Romans, who made extensive use of the metal, as it was plentiful, had a low-boiling point, and was easy to process. Besides dishware, lead was also used in kitchen utensils, jars, liquor bottles, and even water pipes. Some historians therefore have identified lead poisoning as the cause of Rome's eventual downfall.

In the modern era, the invention of stainless steel by Harry Brearley in the early 20th century not only overcame the principal weakness of iron – rust – but in addition produced an alloy which was light and relatively inexpensive. However, stainless steel contains nickel and chromium, which are heavy metals like lead. These metals are not discharged easily once accumulated in the body, even in negligible quantities, and may have negative effects after an extended period.

In contrast, *Bangjja* has been shown to have a beneficial effect on the human body. Anecdotal accounts of its benefits, passed down by Korean housewives, tell us that when dropwort is soaked in a *Bangjja* container, poisonous insects stick to the sides of the dish, making the vegetables easier to clean. One traditional method used to improve the taste of *Kimchi* and other fermented vegetables is to cover the vegetables with straw that has been used to clean the bronzeware. When shaving a monk's head, a knife made from *Bangjja* was also used. This was because even if the knife made a cut by mistake, the wound would not become infected. How can these traditional beliefs be explained?

In November 2003, at the Kyungwon University Department of Foods and Bioengineering, a series of experiments was conducted to investigate the scientific basis of these claims regarding *Bangjja's* properties[23]. Water was poured into 3 containers, made of porcelain, stainless steel, and *Bangjja*, and after 24 hours the properties of the water were tested for changes. The water in the porcelain and stainless steel showed no changes in mineral content, but inside the *Bangjja* small quantities of minerals such as sodium, copper, and zinc were detected. Minerals such as these are an essential part of the human diet, and must be obtained externally, as they are not produced by the body.

---

[23] The findings were broadcast in a documentary on 22 Nov. 2003 by the Korean Broadcasting System (KBS). This can be seen at kscpp.net

Left: *Bangjja* bronzeware   Middle: Porcelain   Right: Stainless steel

Flower Test <11th Day>

In another experiment, flowers were placed inside bowls of porcelain, stainless steel, and *Bangjja*, which were all filled with water. The flowers in the porcelain and stainless steel withered after a week, but the flower inside the *Bangjja* remained fresh. This is because the mineral elements passed on by the *Bangjja* supplied inorganic nutrients to the plant, assisting its biotic activity. Ultimately, the improved taste of *kimchi* and *jangajji* may also be attributed to these mineral elements produced by the bronzeware, which enhance the taste and nutritional value of the fermented foods.

Another experiment demonstrated the ability of *Bangjja* to eradicate the lethal O-157 colon bacillus, which claimed many lives during an outbreak in Japan in 1996. A quantity of O-157 was mixed with distilled water and placed inside containers made of stainless steel, porcelain and *Bangjja*. When the water in the *Bangjja* was tested after 24 hours, not a trace of the original pathogen was discovered, while the bacteria in the other containers remained unaffected. Professor Park from Kyungwon University points out that *Bangjja* dishware has a sterilizing, rather than antibiotic, effect in this case. According to his explanation, pathogens with a high level of toxicity contain many anions (negatively charged ions), and since the copper in the *Bangjja* produces cations (positively charged ions), the pathogens are therefore eliminated, and the water stored in the *Bangjja* comes out cleaner and safer.

The disadvantage of *Bangjja* bronzeware is that it is heavier compared to other forms of tableware and cannot be mass-produced, and it is therefore quite expensive. During the last century, demand for traditional tableware decreased significantly, and it became quite rare in ordinary Korean houses. In the early 21st century, however, the health benefits of *Bangjja* are once again gaining attention. Both beautiful and durable, producing beneficial minerals and neutralizing harmful substances, *Bangjja* is not merely a variety of dishware, but a tangible legacy of enlightened wisdom.

48. *Hanji* Paper

Referred to as 'silk paper' by the Chinese, *Hanji* has been made in Korea for over 1600 years. Stronger than ordinary paper due to the long fibers of mulberry bark, it does not tear easily, is pleasant to the eye and touch, and has found many different uses in household objects, floor and wall papers, shoes, and even armor. Its qualities come not only from its ingredients, but also the long and complex process of making it. It is commonly used as window paper, as it absorbs humidity, and also retains heat more efficiently that glass. The uses of *Hanji* are multiplying, and today extend even to the fields of electronic acoustics (speaker cones), engineering (used as 'muscles' for space probes robots, and shields against electromagnetic interference), and protective clothing (motorcycle helmets).

Hanji, or traditional Korean paper, is an integral part of Korean culture. For more than 1600 years, it has played a central role in the lives of Koreans, who have learned to put it to a great number of uses. In books and handicraft objects, wall and window papers in houses, shoes, and even coffins, *Hanji* was practically an everyday necessity.

Lasting 1000 Years

Hanji is made from the bark of the mulberry or *tak* tree. Because *Hanji* does not rely on acidic chemicals or artificial bleaching methods, it is essentially a 'neutral' paper. Paper made with chemical pulp decays easily and does not last

Naturally Dyed *Hanji* Paper

longer than 200 years. *Hanji* is much more long-lasting, as attested by the old Korean proverb, 'Silk lasts five hundred years, paper a thousand'. In Korea today, there survive four ancient paper manuscripts dating back to the 8th century AD.

Hanji is extremely resilient, yet translucent and smooth to the touch. The paper also resists humidity, and if cured with natural dyes such as dyer's knotweed, safflower, or the amur cork tree, it develops anti-insect and antiseptic properties.

The utility and convenience of *Hanji* have been widely recognized throughout East Asia, and have won the admiration of calligraphers and scholars alike. In *Kao Pan Yu Shi*, Tuyung of the Ming dynasty (1368~1644) says, 'The Koryo paper is white and strong like silk, and when it is written on, the paper absorbs the ink so well that one's affection for it grows naturally.' Because *Hanji* was so refined, the Chinese often mistakenly referred to it as a paper made using silk. Later, during the Yuan dynasty, the Chinese imported paper from Korea for the copying of Buddhist sutras, purchasing as many as 100,000 rolls at one time. The Chinese and Japanese referred to Korean paper by various names, but it was generally recognized as the finest paper available.

How *Hanji* Is Made

Hanji's unique characteristics are based on the natural properties of its raw materials, and the care which is required to make it. The length of the bast-fiber of mulberry bark (8~9mm) is much longer than that of most coniferous trees such as firs, pines or hemlock spruce (3mm), commonly used in chemical pulp, or that of broadleaf trees such as beech, white birch or eukary (1mm). The resilience of the paper is determined largely by the method of manufacture. Thanks to the paper's soft texture and natural fiber patterns, which cannot be reproduced by machines, the time and labor-intensive traditional method has endured.

The Process of Making *Hanji*

1. **Peeling off the bark** - mulberry branches are steamed in cauldrons, and the bark is peeled off.
2. **Washing and bleaching the fiber** - the fibers are steamed in cauldrons and then soaked in running stream water for about three days. After several days, the fibers become bleached. This natural bleaching technique does not damage the fiber and allows the paper to retain the fiber's original, vital luster.
3. **Eliminating impurities** - once the fibers have been bleached, it is essential to remove particles and impurities manually in order to ensure that the *Hanji* is of good quality.
4. **Pulverizing the fiber** - once the impurities have been removed, the fibers are placed on a large stone plate and beaten with a mallet until they become loose. Machines are not used in this stage of the manufacture of *Hanji*, as mechanical blades would damage the fiber.
5. **Dispersing the crushed fiber in water** - the fibers are placed inside a

paper container or tank and mixed well to ensure that they are dispersed evenly.

6. **Addition of mulberry starch** - after pouring the crushed fiber into water, *takpul* (Hibiscus manihot L), also known as mulberry starch, is added as a gluing agent, as its roots secrete a sticky fluid. *Takpul* plays a very important role in making *Hanji*, and it is often grown especially for this purpose. As a water-soluble polysaccharide with cohesive characteristics, mulberry starch helps the mulberry fibers to disperse and float in the water, rather than lump together. By increasing the viscosity, it also slows the flow of liquid over the surface of the screen, giving time to make the sheets thin and even. Finally, it enhances the durability and general appearance of the paper.

7. **Straining the fiber** - Korean papermakers have a unique method of straining the fiber of *hanji* paper. As opposed to the standard 'caged-in' method, whereby the fiber and starch mixture is held in place, and left to be strained without applying motion to the screen, Koreans use a so-called 'dripping' technique. In the Korean method, no covering is used; the fiber and starch mixture is placed on the screen, and is gently shaken side to side. *Hanji* owes its resilience to this dripping method, which allows the mulberry mixture to flow freely in all directions, creating a crisscross pattern, meaning that the paper does not tear easily.

8. **Dehydrating** - the process of dehydration removes the moisture, and allows the sheets to be separated one by one. The sheets must be dried over a long period of time in order to ensure that they separate well. Traditionally, they were dried on rocks, but today, pressurized dehydrating equipment is used.

9. **Drying the paper** - once the sheets have been dehydrated, each one is transferred to the drying surface. There are two methods of drying: sun drying, using wooden boards, and iron plate drying, using a steam-heated

iron surface. The latter method is more efficient, but degrades the quality of the *Hanji* somewhat, as the front and the back of the sheet are subjected to slightly different conditions.

10. **Smoothing the paper** - the dried sheets of *Hanji* are then pounded in order to make their surfaces even. This process is known as *tochim*. Pounding *Hanji* not only compresses the fibers, but also makes the surface smoother and more radiant. This technique for smoothing out the surface of *Hanji* is unique to Korea.

How *Hanji* Is Used

The refined texture and smooth surface of *Hanji* have made it popular among writers and painters for centuries. Brush strokes of ink appear more elegant and profound on *Hanji* paper, and because of its long-lasting qualities, it was often used for the official government records of East Asian dynasties.

The toughness and versatility of *Hanji* have been put to a wide range of uses. A report filed by the financial ministry of Russia toward the end of the Choson dynasty (1392~1910) describes *Hanji* as follows: 'Korean paper is made of fiber, so it is not as weak as that of the West. It is so strong that it can be made into string or cord, and is used in various types of handicraft. The paper is textured, and unless torn along the grain, it does not rip easily, much like cloth.'

In 1683, a report submitted to the king stated, 'Lately it has become fashionable amongst the idler members of society to wear paper-shoes, and as the makers and sellers of such shoes increase in number, the theft of books from noble households is becoming more frequent. This practice must be curbed.' Koreans not only used *hanji* to make wallpaper and floor coverings, but also shoes, sewing boxes, baskets, umbrellas and clothes. *Hanji* could be dyed in many colors, and was used to make purses, cushions, chamber pots, basins,

Window Paper *Changhoji*

dining tables, and other household items. There was even *hanji* armor – a layered paper suit, covered with two-inch deerskin squares fortified with black lacquer. It is said that this armor could not be pierced by arrows.

Amongst its many applications, *Hanji* was most commonly used in traditional Korean homes as window paper (*changhoji*). When applied to latticed windows and doors, it not only assisted ventilation, but also controlled humidity.

In highly humid conditions, it absorbed the moisture to freshen the air, and in dry periods, released it to maintain humidity at an appropriate level.

Hanji also retains heat, as effectively as cotton cloth. In a recent study by Kim Chong-ho, a doctorate in engineering from the University of Perpignan in France, the *changhoji* used in traditional Korean homes was shown to be more heat-efficient than glass windows.

Because *Hanji* is translucent, it allows light into a room. At night, the moonlight shines on *hanji* windows to create a calming, cozy atmosphere. The shadows cast on paper windows and the sound of the wind gently brushing against the paper occupy a special place in the hearts of Korean people.

Rediscovery of *Hanji*

When paper manufacturing became industrialized in the 19th century, traditional Korean paper, which cost so much in time and energy to make, faced the possibility of extinction. However, as the many benefits of *Hanji* become better known, it is re-emerging not only as paper, but as a material with potential for use in many modern fields.

Currently, *Hanji* is most widely used in arts and crafts, for its soft texture, subtle yet vibrant colors, and light yet robust structure. Recently, increasing number of galleries and museums around the Insa-dong district of Seoul have begun to sell *Hanji* items such as jewel boxes, trays, pencil cases, and bags. They also provide *Hanji* craftwork classes.

The *Hanji* lantern, which makes use of the paper's translucent characteristics, is gaining popularity as well. In 2005, the *Hanji* Cultural Festival, introducing *Hanji* clothes and craftworks, was held in Paris. The Parisians showed greatest interest in the colorful *Hanji* lanterns, which appeared in the shape of tigers, turtles, cranes, and lotus flowers.

Hanji Lanterns

The French media also showed great interest in the festival. *Le Nouvel Observateur* was the first to cover it, and gave an account of the public's response to traditional *Hanji*. In an article introducing the Korean tradition of *hanji* and the exhibits of the festival, *Le Figaroscope* wrote, 'Korea's traditional paper has mesmerized France with its magical charm'. The main news programs gave highly positive coverage of the festival and described the shaped lanterns as 'truly fantastic.'

Recently, *Hanji*'s potential uses in the field of engineering are being examined. The Center for Electro-Active Papers Actuator, led by Professor Kim Jae-hwan of Inha University, is currently conducting NASA-funded research into making protective clothing, and even robots for space probes, using *Hanji* paper.

Windows, tables, lanterns and other crafts made of *Hanji* paper

When electricity is passed through the long fibers of *Hanji*, it moves like a muscle. Professor Kim is attempting to apply this phenomenon to robot technology. He asserts that *Hanji*'s unique electric properties and durability can also shield the machine from electromagnetic interference resulting from sunspot activity, and costly space probes may therefore be manufactured using light and inexpensive paper. He believes that if we can make paper objects that move, we can use paper to make tiny robots for surveillance or exploration.

A *Hanji* speaker cone is used in one of the most advanced next generation speaker systems, capable of reproducing sound with the highest degree of accuracy. Until recently, a four channel speaker system (using a tweeter, mid-range driver, woofer, and subwoofer) was considered optimum. Although it was known that an ideal system would combine these four channels in one speaker, this was believed to be possible only in theory. The *Hanji* speaker system has made this theory a reality, perfectly reproducing the four channels using one sheet of *Hanji*. This is possible due to *Hanji*'s high density and its ability to absorb sound.

In addition, because *Hanji* is light, durable, and allows ventilation, it is being considered as a new material for the development of motorcycle and military helmets. As interest in health and well-being increases, interest in the application of *Hanji* in household items or as a construction material has also grown. According to Dr. Cho Hyun-jin of the Korea Forest Research Institute, when *Hanji* is used as wallpaper, its ability to provide ventilation, deodorize, and radiate far infrared light means that it has a positive effect on health. Chon Yongchol, a researcher at the *Hanji* Development Center, says that if *Hanji* is used to make pillows, blankets, or wallpaper, it can reduce the harmful effects of atopic syndrome and dust mites. *Hanji* is also considered an environmentally friendly construction material because it does not become sooty or release toxic gas when burned.

Due to the belief that whatever is traditional is obsolete, *Hanji* was disregarded for many years and remained in obscurity. Today, however, it is re-entering people's lives with renewed vitality.

49. *Kudle*: Traditional Underfloor Heating

Underfloor heating is now used all around the world, and is growing in popularity thanks to its convenience and efficiency. It was re-discovered in the West during modern times by Frank L Wright, who came across the traditional Korean *Kudle* method. An ancient form of heating, the *Kudle* works by means of an outside furnace, underfloor pipes, and a special stone that retains heat for long periods and releases it gradually. The first form of underfloor heating in the world, it was sophisticated enough to be effective, but within the means of both rich and poor to build and use. Still found in Korean homes today, it has been shown to help allergies, aid sleep and improve general quality of life.

In recent years, the use of underfloor heating has become more common around the world. In Germany, Denmark, Austria, and Switzerland, countries that have traditionally relied on convector heating systems such as radiators, nearly half of newly-built homes now have underfloor heating. The reason for the popularity of underfloor heating is the fact that it is noiseless and invisible to the eye, takes up less space, and is more energy-efficient than other forms of heating.

The world's first underfloor heating system

Frank L. Wright of the United States was the first western architect to develop a system of underfloor heating during modern times, using hot water pipes. Creator of the famous Fallingwater and Guggenheim museums, he is regarded as one of the most influential architects of the 20th century.

In his book *The Natural House*, Wright recalls a winter's day in 1914 when he was invited to a client's house in Japan. In a small room, called the 'Korean room,' to which he was led after the meal, he encountered a new form of heating that he had never experienced before. Wright recounted the episode as follows.

> The climate seemed to have changed. No, it wasn't the coffee; it was spring. We were soon warm and happy again – kneeling there on the floor, an indescribable warmth. No heating was visible, nor was it felt directly as such. It was really a matter *not of heating at all* but an affair of *climate*…The Harvard graduate who interpreted for the Baron explained: the Korean room meant a room heated under the floor. The indescribable comfort of being warmed from below was a discovery…There is no other 'ideal' heat. Not even the heat of the sun.
>
> – Frank Lloyd Wright, *The Natural House*, pp. 89-90.

The architect was deeply intrigued by this extraordinary form of heating, whereby warmth radiated from beneath the floor to heat the four corners of the room. He soon afterwards used the concept himself to build hotel baths in Japan, and on his return to the United States, he introduced the same method of heating to his most famous buildings. The system that Wright had experienced in Japan was the *Kudle*, a traditional Korean method of underfloor heating.

Because Korea's history of heating technology goes back to prehistoric times, it is impossible to be precise about the *Kudle*'s date of origin. However, early forms of *Kudle* have been discovered in excavated residential sites from the Old Choson period (BC 2333~BC 108), and academics believe it was used from this time onward.

The word *Kudle* comes from *kueun dol*, which means 'burned stone' in

Korean. Heat is provided by a furnace outside the room, which sends hot air along flues beneath the floor, and the thermal energy is retained by the stone slabs (*Kudle* stone) placed above the flues. This stored energy is released gradually into the room, keeping it warm.

Kudle was mankind's first form of underfloor heating. The Roman *hypocaust* was similar to the *Kudle*, but was used mainly at public bath-houses (*thermae*). It disappeared with the decline of the Roman Empire, and it was not rediscovered until the 19th century.

Thanks to the *Kudle*, everyone in Korea could pass the winter in warmth, whether they lived in the city or the countryside, whether they were wealthy or poor. Horace Allen, an American priest and doctor who visited Korea about a hundred years ago, left the following observations in his book *Things Korean*.

> However humble the hut of the peasant or coolie, it always has its tight little sleeping room, the stone and cement floor of which with its rich brown oil paper covering, is kept nicely warmed by the little fire necessary for cooking the rice twice daily. In this respect these people fare better than do their neighbors, for the Japanese houses are notoriously cold, and a fire pot for warming the fingers is the only native system of heating, while the Chinese never are warm in the raw cold of winter.
>
> – Horace Allen, *Things Korean*, p. 67.

In the case of a traditional *Kudle* heating system, heat from the furnace is transferred to the stone slab (the *Kudle* stone) via a network of flues, with smoke from the fire allowed out through the chimney located at the opposite end. The floor is supported by stone piers, with the *Kudle* stone placed on top. It is then covered with clay, and overlaid with yellow-colored oiled *hanji* flooring-paper.

In Korean homes today, a boiler has taken the place of the furnace, and metal

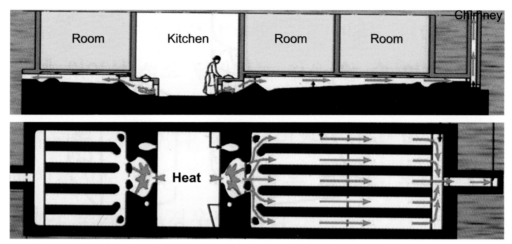

Side view (above) and ground plan (below) of the traditional *Kudle* system

pipes carry out the function of the flues. Instead of burning fuel, warm water from the boiler is circulated to heat the rooms. Though much may have changed in terms of outward appearance, so far as principle and structure are concerned, the concept has remained virtually the same.

The World's First Smokeless Heating

In Europe, until the 12th and 13th centuries, people and livestock lived under the same roof, contributing body heat to one another. At the center of the house was a fire pit for the lighting of an open fire, which was used for cooking and heating. Sometimes the fireplace was put on a raised platform made of stone or brick, but until as late as the Middle Ages, most households lacked a specific ventilation system such as a chimney. When a fire was lit, the entire house would be filled with smoke.

In certain parts of Europe, roofs were constructed in a funnel shape to let the smoke escape. These features were known as 'Rauchschlot' in Germany and Austria, and in mountainous regions such as the Alps, they can still be seen in houses dating from the 17th and 18th centuries.

Though houses with Rauchschlot solved the problem of excessive smoke, the quality of heating suffered, as the heat escaped from the house along with the smoke. To live in the cold without smoke, or to live in warmth and endure the smoke, was a perpetual dilemma.

By means of the *Kudle* system, Korean homes were able to enjoy the best of both worlds. Traditional examples of *Kudle* are relatively well preserved today in the Royal Palaces of Korea. As it was believed that that no smoke should be seen in the King's place of residence, the furnace was hidden beneath the building. To minimize the amount of fire and smoke, charcoal was used instead of firewood. Chimneys were also placed far away from the King's sight, and the distance between the furnace and chimney became very great as a result, with a minimum distance of 28 meters.

The World's First Heat Storage System

An open fire or fireplace may be warm while it is lit, but as soon as the fire goes out, the heat quickly disappears. On the other hand, because the *Kudle* is a form of heating which retains thermal energy in the *Kudle* stone beneath the floor, the room can be kept warm for long periods without the need to create further heat.

In the grounds of the Chilbulsa Temple in Kyongsang Province, there is a famous building called Ajabang which is said to have kept warm for a month and half (100 days in other accounts) after just one heating. Tradition has it that in the reign of the Silla King Hyo-gong (r. 897-912), a Buddhist master called Tamgong built a specially designed *Kudle* so that even in the depth of winter, practitioners could keep warm and devote themselves single-mindedly to inner cultivation. Master Tamgong's *Kudle* was unfortunately destroyed by fire during the Korean War. It was restored in the 1980's, but modern technicians were not

An ornate chimney at Changdok Palace

able to replicate the millennium-old structure completely. The warmth from one heating now lasts for around a week.

The secret of the lasting warmth of the *Kudle* lies in the stone itself - mica. Mica is a mineral commonly found in igneous and metamorphic rocks. The 'white' variety of mica can withstand temperatures of 400~500°C, and because its thermal conductivity is low, it retains heat for a long time and releases it gradually. Also, being an alkaline rock rich in minerals such as magnesium oxide and calcium, when heat is applied, it emits a large amount of far-infrared radiation. Far-infrared radiation has a longer wavelength than visible light, and due to its high thermal conductivity, it is widely used in natural health treatments such as thermal therapies.

Kudle, Warming the Body and Mind

When a fire is lit, the flames naturally point upwards. They may be blown to the side by a gust of wind, but they always return when the wind calms. Similarly, smoke and heat both rise upwards. The *Kudle* is a system of heating which aims to mirror this principle of nature.

Fireplaces, iron stoves or radiators are all designed to supply heat horizontally, and are therefore less able to provide heat efficiently. Moreover, since the heated air rises upwards, one's head can become uncomfortably hot, sometimes causing a headache, while our lower body does not receive the heat and remains cold. In underfloor heating, because the heat rises from the floor, which is the lowest point in the room, every part of the room is evenly heated. Also, as our feet touch the warm floor, the blood vessels are stimulated, helping circulation.

Another advantage of underfloor heating is hygiene. With ordinary floors, carpets are used, and outdoor shoes are worn inside. The air inside becomes easily polluted from the dirt, dust and germs picked up from outside. With the

Kudle system, neither carpets nor shoes are required, and one can live in comfort and health upon the traditional *hanji* (Korean handmade paper) floor.

Most importantly, the *Kudle* fulfils the primary purpose of heating, namely keeping the interior warm. However long a fire is lit, one can only be warm when close to it, and as soon as the fire is out, the room grows cold again. Even when standing next to the fireplace, one has to turn constantly to warm the back as well as the front. Hence the saying, "However large the fireplace, it is never too large."

A German princess Liselotte von der Pfalz, notes in her letter home in 1695 that 'the water and wine have frozen at the King's table,' later writing in 1701 that 'All that keeps me warm at night are the six small dogs I take with me to bed.' Thanks to the *Kudle*, even a poor peasant in Korea could live in far greater warmth than any king in Europe. Reverend J.S. Gale, who lived in Korea as a missionary from 1889 to 1896, describes his experiences in his book, *Korean Sketch*, as follows.

> Sleeping in a small Korean hut I found, at first, to be one of my hardest trials. In a tight room, without one particle of ventilation, the floor heated nearly to the frying point, you spread your blanket. The inexperienced traveler, pursued by fiery dreams, baked almost brown, gasps for breath and wishes for the morning. But after a year or two of practice, one gets to like the hot floor, for as the natives say, it lets you out after a cold day's journey.
>
> – James Gale, *Korean Sketches*, p. 134.

In several places throughout the book, he likens the *Kudle* to a 'frying fan floor,' and speaks of his ordeals trying to sleep inside the rooms heated to a point far beyond comfortable warmth. This would have perhaps been due to the Korean custom of lighting a larger fire than usual upon receiving a guest.

Underfloor heating has spread to many places in the world today, from China to Japan, across the Middle East to Europe, warming people's bodies and minds. Aseda Kazumi, a researcher at Tokyo Gas, which provides underfloor heating services in Japan, says that clients have often told him stories of how allergies have disappeared, how they sleep better at night, and even how their families have started to come back home early for the pleasure and comfort of underfloor heating.

When the body is warm and comfortable, the mind naturally becomes warm and happy too. There may be many advantages to underfloor heating, but the warmth and happiness of the mind is its greatest benefit.

Traditional Korean Room

50. The World's First 'Active' Greenhouse

Greenhouses have existed since ancient times. It was not known until recently, that the first greenhouse conforming to modern standards – allowing for adjustment of air and soil temperature – was built in Korea during the 15th century AD. The greenhouse described in the *Sanga Yorok* has recently been successfully reconstructed, and combines traditional Korean heating technology with sophisticated features ensuring heat retention and control of condensation.

People first began to build greenhouses around 2,200 years ago in order to protect plants from exposure to extreme weather conditions. In the East, a greenhouse made with paper is said to have existed during the reign of Emperor Qin Shi Huang in 221 BC, and in the West, it is recorded that the Emperor Nero had a greenhouse made out of granite in order to grow crops in 42 BC. These early greenhouses depended on natural light, and would in today's terminology be called 'passive' greenhouses.

'Active' greenhouses – in which it is possible for the temperature to be increased or decreased manually – appeared much later. According to a historical study of greenhouse development by the Dutch horticulturalist Muijzenberg, the earliest example of an active greenhouse appeared in Heidelberg, Germany, in 1619, in which the internal temperature was altered by means of a stove. In 1691, an air heating system was installed inside a greenhouse in England, and is traditionally regarded as the first step in the development of today's active greenhouses.

In 2001, a member of Korea's National Heritage Trust discovered a book entitled *Sanga Yorok* in an antique bookshop. He later remarked that he had bought the book simply for its old appearance, being an amateur collector. The book subsequently came to the attention of Han Bok-ryeo, a researcher in the field of traditional royal cuisine, and Professor Kim Wong-won, a horticulturalist. They identified the book as the nation's oldest surviving manual of farming and cookery techniques. It was written in the year 1450 AD by the medical officer Chon Sun-ui, during the reign of King Sejong. Remarkably, the book contained descriptions of a greenhouse conforming to sophisticated modern standards. *Sanga Yorok* explains the process by which it was built in a chapter entitled 'Growing Vegetables During Winter':

> First of all, construct an enclosure of an appropriate size. The northern, eastern, and western sides of the enclosure should be opaque, and covered with oiled-paper. Install a lattice-window in the wall that faces south, and cover it with oiled-paper also. Lay the *kudle* stone, taking care that no smoke is allowed to escape from beneath it. Deposit soil to a height of 1½ *ja*, and plant spring vegetables. Ensure that no wind enters at night, and when the weather is very cold, always cover the building with a thick *bigae* [a straw-mat used for agricultural purposes], and remove it immediately when the cold has abated. Water the soil every day to ensure that it does not become dry. Place a cauldron outside, and connect it to the room using a long tube. Boil the cauldron each evening, so that the steam from the cauldron keeps the room comfortably warm.

The greenhouse described in this book was designed to regulate the temperature and humidity requirements of plants and crops in a very precise manner. Heat was supplied by means of a *kudle,* a traditional Korean method of heating. The oiled *hanji* paper made it possible to raise the inner temperature and control ventilation and humidity. However, the extent to which these methods alone could regulate the temperature was limited. The additional inflow of steam from the cauldron had the effect of raising both the temperature and humidity.

One feature of the greenhouse that particularly impressed horticulturalists and academics is the process by which the *kudle* would automatically raise the temperature of the soil as the boiling water from the cauldron warmed the air. Even if the air inside was warm, if the soil was not warm enough, the growth of the plants would be slower. The importance of keeping the roots of a plant warm was therefore understood in Korea during the 15th century.

On 22 February 2002, after much preparation and research, a successful attempt was made to rebuild the world's first active greenhouse, as recorded in the *Sanga Yorok*. The floor of the restored greenhouse measured 26m², and the roof was angled southwards to maximize exposure to natural light.

Shortly after its completion on 3 March 2002, Professor Kim of Kyemyeong Cultural University planted six vegetables (radish, lettuce, Chinese cabbage, wild rocambole, spinach, and chard), and monitored the temperature and humidity levels of the greenhouse over a space of 20 days. Initially, the subterranean temperature outside was 8.6°C, too low for plant growth, while the soil inside the greenhouse was at an ideal temperature of 26°C. The radish and lettuce sprouted after three days, the other vegetables soon afterwards, and after two weeks they had all grown to full size. Potted hydrangea and pear trees were also grown in the greenhouse, blooming two months earlier than usual.

The inner temperature was measured four times a day (6 a.m., 1 p.m., 6 p.m., 10 p.m.) at various points inside the greenhouse. The soil above the *kudle* always remained at 20°C or higher, and the air temperature at 10°C minimum. During the night, the soil temperature inside and outside differed by more than 25°C, proving that the greenhouse was generating adequate heat. Although humidity was as low as 40% at the hottest time of the day (1 p.m), it was otherwise kept at 70%, a level suitable for growth.

Exterior and Interior of the reconstructed 15th century greenhouse

The material used for the walls of the greenhouse was also important. Solar heat enters a greenhouse by means of 'incident' solar rays, and escapes by means of 'long', or infrared, solar rays. An ideal material for insulation will therefore have a high transmission ratio for incident solar rays, and low one for infrared rays. Moreover, the material must diffuse a large proportion of the transmitted rays, and its tensile and tear strength should be high. Also, as droplets of condensation will form on the surface of the walls, the material must be able to retain them, allowing them to flow down to the floor. This is necessary to prevent them falling directly on to the plants, and potentially causing damage or introducing impurities.

Oiled *hanji* fulfilled all of these criteria. Because oil particles fill the gaps in the structure of the fabric, oiled *hanji* does not refract the light but allows it to pass straight through, resulting in a high transmission ratio. Moreover, its tensile and tear strength are greater than that of vinyl or unoiled *hanji*, and water droplets that form on the surface of the paper travel along its surface to the ground.

In August 2002, at the 26th International Horticultural Congress in Toronto, Professor Jeon Hui of the Korean National Horticultural Research Institute informed scholars from across the world about the discovery of *Sanga Yorok* and the reconstruction of the greenhouse. Also present at the Congress was Professor Paul Nelson of North Carolina State University, the author of *Greenhouse Operation & Management*, a widely-used manual in the field of horticulture. He learned for the first time of Korea's 15th century greenhouse at the Congress, and said that he would rewrite the history of the greenhouse in the forthcoming revised edition of his book.

Thanks to the discovery of a single volume in the corner of an old bookshop, forgotten for hundreds of years, the horticultural world has discovered a missing chapter in its history.

Science and Technology in the 21st Century Korea

Today South Korea is playing an important role in the world, particularly in the area of science and technology research. The country has an advanced IT infrastructure, and two of its largest conglomerates, Samsung and LG, are world leaders in electronics, semiconductors, computers, and mobiles phones. Home to the world's third largest steel producer, POSCO, it is the world's largest shipbuilder, the world's fourth largest oil refiner, and one of the top five automobile producers.

It is also prominent in the fields of biotechnology, nanotechnology, artificial intelligence, construction, engineering, petrochemicals, and textiles. Korea has space partnership with Russia, and has launched the Arirang-1 and Arirang-2 satellites, used for geographical and environmental observation. In the field of renewable energy, South Korean scientists at the Gwangju Institute of Science and Technology have collaborated with the University of California in Santa Barbara to develop an organic photovoltaic power cell with a power-conversion efficiency of 6.5%. The sophisticated consumer base of Korea makes it an ideal testing ground for new products, and it is one of the first markets in which global giants such as Microsoft and Motorola carry out trials before launching products globally.

The following are some of Korea's most recent achievements, which have featured in major journals and media channels around the world, including the New York Times, *Time*, *Nature*, and the BBC.

Telecommunications

In 2007, a book called *Digital Korea* was published in Britain. According to its synopsis, it describes "a country where every household internet connection has already been upgraded to broadband; where 100 Mb/s speeds are already sold and gigabit speeds already coming; where every phone sold is a cameraphone; where three out of every four mobile subscriptions is a 3G connection; where cars and PCs and mobile phones now ship with in-built digital TVs; where 42% of the population maintain a blogsite and four out of ten have created an avatar of themselves; where over half of the population pay with cellphones and 25% of the total South Korean population have participated inside a multiplayer online game, in fact inside the same multiplayer online game."

South Korea is the most wired, and wirelessly connected, information society in the world. After the 1997 financial crisis, a conscious decision was made to transform the country into a high-tech powerhouse. Korea has since achieved many firsts in the field of IT. It was the first country to make high-speed internet available in every school. At present an astonishing 72 percent of all households have broadband internet access.

Two Korean inventions, Wireless Broadband Internet (WiBro) and Digital Multimedia Broadcasting (DMB) technologies, have established the country as a global leader in digital convergence services. KT Corp., Korea's largest fixed-line telephony and internet service provider, launched WiBro commercially in the area of Seoul for the first time in the world in 2006, making it possible for internet users to remain online wherever they went. Normally, Wireless Local Area Network (WLAN) services require hot spots with fixed antennae, and service is confined to a specific area. However, WiBro allows people to enjoy the benefits of a wireless service anywhere at broadband speeds, which is not yet possible with other technologies. In October 2007, the International Telecommunication Union (ITU), a global policymaking group, held a meeting in Geneva in which it classified WiBro technology as the sixth 3G communications standard.

Digital multimedia broadcasting (DMB) is a system whereby multimedia (radio, TV and datacasting) are transmitted to mobile devices such as mobile phones. The world's first official mobile TV service appeared in South Korea in May 2005, and Korean DMB technology has been adopted as the European standard.

In 2007, the ITU conducted a study in association with the United Nations (UN), and after considering 180 countries concluded for the second year running that South Korea ranked highest in terms of the digital opportunity index (DOI). The DOI is an important indicator of the degree of a country's IT development, taking 11 factors into account, such as the standard of IT infrastructure, and the affordability of communications technology relative to income.

Artificial Intelligence

Faced with critically low birth rates and an ageing population, South Korea is turning to robots to offset the growing decline in the workforce. In 2005, the Korea Advanced Institute of Science and Technology (KAIST) developed the world's second walking humanoid robot, called Albert Hubo. Honda's Asimo

(Left) Hubo reading newspaper (Right) Hubo shaking hands with President Bush

and KAIST's Hubo models are currently the only robots of their kind.

With a head resembling that of the famous physicist Albert Einstein, the robot drew international attention in November 2005 during the Asia-Pacific Economic Cooperation forum, where it greeted world leaders. Hubo can dance, perform Tai Chi, display more than 48 facial expressions, recognize human faces and speech, and hold realistic conversations. According to Professor Oh Jun-ho of KAIST, Hubo's functionality is enhanced by Frubber, a spongelike silicon-based material, special cameras installed in the robot's eyes, and powerful artificial intelligence software.

In 2006, scientists from the Korean University of Science and Technology unveiled the world's second female android capable of expressing human emotions, called Ever-1. Future versions of this model are expected to walk, sing, dance, read stories to children, and be used in homes, museums, and departments stores. In the same year, the Intelligent Surveillance and Guard Robot was built, a sentry robot capable of detecting and repelling intruders along the heavily-armored border with North Korea.

Biotechnology

The South Korean biotechnology industry has developed from being a fast-follower to an innovator thanks to extensive R&D networks based on cooperation between industry, universities, and research institutes. Outstanding infrastructure, groundbreaking research publications, and a growing number of patents all attest to the high standard of Korean biotechnology.

Korea's capabilities in the field of genetics were demonstrated in 2005 with the appearance of Snuppy, the world's first cloned dog, the most advanced and complex cloning procedure ever performed at the time. Since then, two females of an endangered wolf species have been cloned by the Seoul National

University team.

Thanks to these advances, it is now possible for cloning to take place on a commercial basis. In February 2008, a Californian woman whose pet dog had recently died sent a tissue sample to a Korean biotech company, requesting five identical clones at a cost of 50,000 US dollars. The woman had been devoted to her dog ever since 1996 when it had saved her from being attacked by another dog three times its size. Since she was disabled and confined to a wheel chair, the dog had been a great companion to her, and assisted her with everyday tasks for ten years.

Construction

Korean construction companies are among the limited number worldwide capable of offering Engineering Procurement Construction (EPC) contracts, turnkey arrangements that encompass all aspects of the building process from design to project finance. Amongst many other projects, Samsung C&T Corporation's iconic super-tower, Burj Dubai, currently nearing completion in the United Arab Emirates, is one of the most outstanding examples.

Expected to be the world's tallest building, its precise height has not yet been revealed, but it is expected to be at least 700 meters high, nearly twice the height of the Empire State Building, and 200 meters taller than the current tallest building, the Taipei 101 in Taiwan. The 55-story Emirates Towers Dubai Hotel and 73-story Raffles City Complex in Singapore, both built by Ssangyong Engineering & Construction, and Samsung's 88-story Petronas Twin Towers in Malaysia, completed in 1998, are also famous architectural landmarks.

Doosan Heavy Industries & Construction, a South Korean water plant builder, has developed an unrivaled leadership in its field. Doosan holds a 42 percent share of the worldwide market for water desalination, and expects to earn at least

Burj Dubai

$40 billion over the next 20 years from sales to the six countries of the Arabian Peninsula – United Arab Emirates, Oman, Qatar, Kuwait, Jordan, and Saudi Arabia. Building on its success in the Middle East, it is now planning to expand into other regions such as North America and Africa.

Bibliography

Sources in Korean

김근배 외, 『한국 과학기술 인물 12인』, 해나무, 2005.

김남응, 『구들 이야기, 온돌 이야기』, 단국대학교 출판부, 2004.

김동욱, 『실학 정신으로 세운 조선의 신도시 수원화성』, 돌베개, 2002.

김맑아, 『과학자도 놀란 창덕궁의 비밀』, 『과학동아』, 2007년 2월호

남문현, 『장영실과 자격루: 조선시대 시간측정 역사 복원』, 서울대학교 출판부, 2002.

남천우, 『유물의 재발견』, 학고재, 1997.

문중양, 『우리역사 과학기행』, 동아시아, 2006.

박선희, 『한국 고대 복식: 그 원형과 정체』, 지식산업사, 2002.

박성래, 『측우기는 왜 중국의 발명품이 되었나』, 『내일을 여는 역사』 18 호 (2004 년 겨울).

박종철 편, 『김치과학』, 푸른세상, 2007.

박창범, 『하늘에 새긴 우리 역사』, 김영사, 2002.

손보기, 『금속활자와 인쇄술』, 세종대왕기념사업회, 2000.

손제하, 『선조들이 우리에게 물려준 고대 하이테크 100가지』, 일빛, 2000.

신동원, 『조선사람 허준』, 한겨레신문사, 2001.

———, 『우리 과학의 수수께끼』, 한겨레출판, 2006.

이승철, 『우리가 정말 알아야 할 우리 한지』, 현암사, 2002.

이종호, 『세계 최고의 우리 문화유산』, 컬처라인, 2001.

———, 『한국 7대 불가사의』, 역사의 아침, 2007.

이효지, 『한국의 음식문화』, 신광출판사, 1998.

임재해 외, 『고대에도 한류가 있었다』, 지식산업사, 2007.

전상운, 『한국과학사』, 사이언스북스, 2000.

정동찬 외, 『겨레과학인 우리 공예』, 민속원, 1999

채연석 • 강사임, 『우리의 로켓과 화약무기』, 서해문집, 1998.

최준식, 『한국인에게 밥은 무엇인가』, 휴머니스트, 2004.

한국콩박물관건립추진위원회 편, 『콩』, 고려대학교출판부, 2005.

Sources in English

Allen, Horace Newton, *Things Korean*, Fleming H. Revell Company, 1908.

Chen, Bing-Huei, 'Formation of Cholesterol Oxidation Products in Marinated Foods during Heating', *Journal of Agriculture and Food Chemistry,* American Chemical Society, Volume 54, 2006.

Gale, James Scarth, *Korean Sketches*, Fleming H. Revell Company, 1898.

Jeon, Sang-woon, *A History of Science in Korea*, Jimoondang Publishing Company, 1998.

Messina, M. J. 'Soyfoods: Their Roles in Disease Prevention and Treatment', *Soybeans, Chemistry, Technology, and Utilization*, Chapman and Hall, 1997.

Muizenberg, Erwin, *A History of Greenhouses*, Institute for Agricultural Engineering, Wageningen, Netherlands, 1980.

Needha, Joseph., Ling, Wang, *Science and Civilisation in China, Volume 4, Physics and Physical Technology*, Cambridge at the University Press, 1965.

Kim-Renaud, Young-Key, *King Sejong the Great: The Light of Fifteenth Century Korea*, International Circle of Korean Linguistics, 1997.

Park, Changbom, *Astronomy: Traditional Korean Science*, Ewha Womans University Press, 2007.

Various authors, *Korean Cultural Heritage- Fine Arts*, The Korea Foundation, 1994.

Wright, Frank, *The Natural House*, New York: Horizon Press, 1970.

Published by Korean Spirit & Culture Promotion Project

Korean Spirit & Culture Promotion Project is a 501(c)(3) not for profit organization that was formed under the Diamond Sutra Recitation Group (Chungwoo Buddhist Foundation) in October 2005 to promote Korean history and culture. KSCPP has been publishing and distributing free booklets and DVDs on Korean heritage. Please direct all inquries to kscpp@diamondsutra.org.

New York
158-16 46th Ave., Flushing, NY 11358
☎ 718-539-9108
New Jersey
190 Mountain Rd, Ringoes, NJ 08551
☎ 609-333-9422
Los Angeles
2197 Seaview Dr, Fullerton, CA 92833
☎ 562-644-8949
Atlanta
2100 Bishop Creek Drive, Marietta,
GA 30062 ☎ 770-640-1284

South Korea
131-80 Seongbuk 2 dong, Seongbuk-gu
Seoul 136-824
☎ 82-2-742-0172
Germany
Hiltistr, 7a 86916 Kaufering
☎ 49-8191-70618
United Kingdom
57 Amberwood Rise, New Malden,
Surrey KT3 5JQ
☎ 44-208-942-1640

* When you finish this booklet, please donate it to a library or school so that it can be shared with others. It would also be greatly appreciated if you could leave your comments and impressions in the guestbook at www.kscpp.net or www.koreanhero.net. Thank you.

Korean Spirit and Culture Website

www.kscpp.net

All booklets published in the series are available on our website, as well as additional materials covering various aspects of Korean history and culture.

Published so far:

Admiral Yi Sun-sin

King Sejong the Great

Chung Hyo Ye

Fifty Wonders of Korea

Taste of Korea

Online video library includes:

Korean Cuisine

Hanbok, the Clothes of Nature

Traditional Dance and Music

A Sparking Journey to Korea

UNESCO World Heritage in Korea

And more…